TRAVEL GUIDE to BRITISH/AMERICAN ENGLISH

Norman Moss

PASSPORT BOOKS

Trade Imprint of National Textbook Company
Lincolnwood, Illinois U.S.A.

By the same author:
Men Who Play God: The Story of the Hydrogen Bomb
The Pleasures of Deception
The Politics of Uranium

1987 Printing

This edition first published in 1986 by Passport Books, Trade
Imprint of National Textbook Company, 4255 West Touhy
Avenue, Lincolnwood, Illinois 60646-1975 U.S.A.
Manufactured in the United States of America.

6 7 8 9 0 ML 9 8 7 6 5 4 3 2

Travel Guide to British/American English

Norman Moss was born in Britain, but brought up mostly in the United States. He returned to Britain at the age of nineteen with such a marked American accent that English friends took to calling him "Tex," and he has been culturally bilingual, not to say schizophrenic, ever since.

He has worked as a journalist for both British and American media, including Reuters and the Associated Press, and has traveled widely as a foreign correspondent for an American radio network. He is the author of three other books. He lives in London.

Contents

Acknowledgements

The individuals who have helped me are too many to name. Most of my friends and many passing acquaintances have found themselves interrogated at one time or another on their use and understanding of certain words. Some allowed themselves to be formed into panels. Among those who contributed particularly or provided specialized knowledge are: Professor Ruby Cohn of the University of California; Norman and Barbara Gelb; Richard Lanman of the Marine Midland Bank; Robert and Donna McDonald; Ron Pollard of Ladbroke's, the bookmakers; and Alan Taylor, do-it-yourself author.

Many people wrote to me after the first edition appeared with suggestions for additions or emendations. David Singmaster, an American mathematics lecturer at the South London Polytechnic with an eclectic store of knowledge, generously loaned me his own extensive notes on the two languages, and these proved useful; and Katsuei Yamagishi, who has translated this dictionary into Japanese, contributed from his remarkable knowledge of the English language.

Finally, this book owes much to my wife Hilary, who acted as a constant sounding-board on English as the true-bred British understand it, and alphabetized the text.

INTRODUCTION

This book is intended primarily to help Britons and Americans understand one another better and communicate with one another more easily. The need for such a book has occurred to me often as I watched some Anglo-American misunderstanding caused by the difference in vocabularies. Such as seeing an American trying to get a martini in a British pub, or a corned beef sandwich in a restaurant. Or the time I heard an American student at Cambridge University telling some English friends how he climbed over a locked gate to get into his college and tore his pants, and one of them asked, "But, how could you tear your pants without tearing your trousers?" (In England, *pants* are *underpants*!)

The book lists those words that are different in the two languages in their common usage. The criterion is whether a word is familiar to most people in one country or the other, not whether it is listed in a dictionary. There are words listed in Webster's that are in use in Britain but are hardly heard in America, and some in the Oxford English Dictionary that have not been heard in conversation in Britain for decades. And Webster's may not be much help to an Englishman who finds himself in difficulties with some of Tom Wolfe's baroque American, or Richard Pryor's humor.

Some words in one language are unknown in the other, like Britain's *Bath chair* (wheelchair), *loo* (toilet), and *panda car* (police patrol car), and America's *bobbie pin*, *highball*, and *piker*. Others have different meanings that can cause misunderstandings, like *dormitory*, *cot*, and *tights*. In Britain, dormitory means a room, not a building. Dormitories housing male and female students would indicate a shocking situation to an Englishman. A cot is a bed for a small child; tights means hose or pantyhose, not ballet tights. There are a few that even have the opposite meaning in the other language, like *enjoin* (to compel), *public school* (private school), and *table* (as a verb). Table means to put down for discussion, not to set aside as in America. This one word has led to much misunderstanding in business and political meetings. Words in the first category cause incomprehension: those in the last two may cause trouble, because the difference can create situations in which people think they understand one another when they don't. I saw a minor instance of this recently when I attended a lecture in London given by a senior figure in the American nuclear power industry. He talked about measures which delayed the construction of nuclear power plants for electrical utilities, and said these meant increased rates. The Britons in the audience nodded, for this made perfect sense; but it was the wrong sense. They did not really understand him, and he did not know that *rates* means local property taxes in Britain.

I have tried to give here not only the meaning of a word, but also, where appropriate, the verbal or social context in which it is likely to be used. Most Americans know roughly what the word *bloody* means in Britain, but not when they can safely use it.

Since the criterion for inclusion is what is commonly heard, it leaves much room for disagreement. Heard by whom? Language varies by age, occupation, social group, and geography. In the case of some words, the linguistic dividing line is not the Atlantic but age; young people on both sides use terms in common that are alien to their parents. Most of the language coming out of the pop music world is international, as are the attitudes that go with it.

A word that is foreign to one person will not be foreign to another. New Yorkers, Washingtonians, and Bostonians hear more words from Britain than Westerners. Americans who go to the theater and to foreign movies regularly are more likely to hear British-English words than those who do not. Some people may inherit words from Britain through their family. Any reader may find words listed here as belonging to the other language that are familiar. The chances are that they are not familiar to others.

Questions of what words do and do not belong in both languages are complicated by the speed with which the two languages are changing, both within themselves and in relation to one another. Words go out of use and others arise constantly. *Glitch* and *grunt* (American) and *gazump* and *suss* (British) are recent arrivals, but will be around for a long time. Some service terms that made the transition to civilian life after World War II and were much used in the next two decades or so are heard only rarely today, words such as *gen* and *line-shoot* in Britain and *sad sack* and *scuttlebutt* in America.

In America, words associated with drug fashions have now emerged into the mainstream of the language. People who never touch even the softest drugs now talk happily about being *spaced out* and *hyping up* something. Young people reach out for their colloquialisms into black slang, and come out with words like *bad* and *paper* in their new meanings. The counterpart in Britain is a reaction against gentility. Very visible in accents and clothes, this is seen also in vocabulary, for instance, in the adoption of words that are or are imagined to be underworld slang like *suss out* and *bent*.

The two languages are moving closer together. The accents, speech rhythms and words of each country are becoming more familiar to the other. Increased travel across the Atlantic both ways is a factor. Others are the growing number of British programs shown on US television—there have always been a lot of American shows on the British airwaves—the wide circulation in Britain of American magazines, and the use of film from British publishers to reprint books published in America and vice versa.

The movement of words is mostly eastwards. Every year, more and more words that were exclusively American are found in the written and spoken language of both countries. A generation ago, the use in Britain of the word *guy* or *campus* would stamp one as an American or Canadian, but today these words fall from the most purely British lips. The sexual term to *lay*, whereas it is not used much in Britain, has now become familiar enough for the village of Llay, near the Welsh border, to decline to send a Miss Llay to a county beauty contest.

Some words have been dropped from the American British section of this book since the first edition was published because, although they were American words then, they have since become common to both languages: words such as *hooker*, *macho*, *ID card*, and *rip-off*. This process of the absorption of American words into the British language has been going on for a long time.

Almost as soon as the British colonies were established in North America, the colonists took new words into their speech, some of them Indian words, some from neighboring settlers who spoke different languages, which in those days meant Dutch (*boodle*, *stoop*, *dumb*), and French (*Indian brave*, *chowder*, *levee*). Later Americans picked up words from Spanish when the nation moved westwards, and from other languages as they were brought in by new kinds of immigrants.

Noah Webster, in whose name American dictionaries are published today, recognized this process when he wrote in the introduction to his first American dictionary, in 1789: "Numerous local causes, such as a new country, new associations of people, new combinations of ideas in arts and science, and some intercourse with tribes wholly unknown in Europe will introduce new words into the American tongue." This forecast was correct; the one that followed in the next sentence was not: "These causes will produce in the course of time a language in N. America as different from the future language of England as the modern Dutch, Danish, and Swedish are from the German or from one another." Webster underrated the amount of social intercourse across the Atlantic which would ensure that the two languages and some of their speakers were in constant contact, not only in the days of universal Dallas and jet travel, but from the earliest days of the American nation.

Even before Noah Webster started compiling his dictionary, words and expressions came back to England from its colonies in America and infiltrated the language of the mother country. Words such as *bluff* (meaning a feature of the landscape), *canoe* and *squatter* traveled over from America in the eighteenth century a little while after the potato and the turkey. H. L. Mencken, in his book *The American Language*, lists American terms that were used by such quintessentially English writers of the Victorian period as Dickens and Thackeray, almost certainly in ignorance of their origin. It is indeed surprising how quickly immigrant words become integrated, the recent arrival and place of origin forgotten. Very few Britons today using the words *doodle*, *fan*, or *grapevine* realize that they came from America in the 1930s, and were almost unknown in Britain before then. Some other words in common use in Britain, such as *flashpoint*, *gimmick*, and *phony* are more recent arrivals still.

Usually, the importation of American words into Britain has encountered a linguistic snobbery that is only part of the cultural snobbery that so bedevilled Anglo-American relations for a long time. In the eighteenth century, Samuel Johnson, writing as a lexicographer, dismissed "the American dialect" as a corruption of English. Frederick Marryat, the author of *Mr. Midshipman Easy*, who followed the custom of so many Victorian authors of visiting America and publishing a diary of his travels, wrote: "It is remarkable how debased the language has become after a short period in America." In 1930, Sir Alfred Knox, a Conservative member of parliament, called in the House of Commons for a limit on the importation of American films, explaining: "The words and accent are disgusting, and there can be no doubt that such films are an evil influence on our language." And, speaking of films, it was only a few years ago that, when Marlon Brando played Napoleon in the film *Desirée*, some English critics remarked loftily on the risibility of seeing Napoleon speaking American phrases in an American accent. It was left to a letter-writer to the London *Times* to point out that Napoleon using British phrases in a British accent would have been no less anomalous, since he actually spoke French.

Mark Twain responded to British pretensions to linguistic superiority in the cocky tone of the successful upstart. "The King's English is not the King's. It's a joint stock company, and Americans own most of the shares," he wrote in *Pudd'nhead Wilson's Journal*. A few other writers since then have felt the need to emphasize the separateness of the American language, as well as of American literature.

Today there is no such pattern of attack and justification. There is, in Britain little pretension to linguistic superiority, and a wide acceptance on both sides that the language is a shared property and heritage. Britain is neither chauvinist nor culturally isolationist. The age of the common man favors the American language and the American style (culturally, as distinct from politically; the Left in Britain has always been pro-American). In fact, it is now chic to use American terms in a way that, in another age, it was chic to use French terms. Shaggy-haired urban hillbillies proclaim that a new record is "real funky, man," while in television studios and advertising offices, thrusting young men say, "No way" and express admiration for each other's *chutzpah*.

I found an interesting confirmation of the prestige status of American terminology in Britain recently when I met the organizer of a group called Prostitutes United for Social and Sexual Integration. I asked her why, since she clearly intended her organization to be taken seriously, she gave it this name, devised that the acronym is PUSSI. (If the British reader needs a translation, it is in the American/British section.) She said that though *pussy* as a sexual colloquialism is American, it is used in Britain by people *in the business*. And she added: "It's an elitist word." Which left me reflecting that one person's elite is another person's lower depths.

On the other hand, words associated with more humdrum, domestic activities, the words of the kitchen and the handyman's cellar, tend to stay on their own side of the Atlantic. *Gripewater*, *paraffin*, and *muslin* are still foreign words to Americans, *apple butter* and *shellac* to Britons. To most people in Britain, a joint is still something you roast rather than something you smoke.

Generalizations about the two languages are as risky and prone to exceptions as are generalizations about the two peoples, but I'll risk a few observations.

British speech tends to be less general, and directed more, in its nuances of meaning, at a sub-group of the population. This can become kind of code, in which few words are spoken because each, along with its attendant murmurings and pauses, carries a wealth of meaning that rests on shared assumptions and attitudes. No pauses are more pregnant than these British pauses. When a Cockney reacts to a situation with a loaded "Ay aye . . ." or a girl from an upper-crust family with "After all, it's a bit much, isn't it?" the speaker assumes that the listener's background and reactions must be so similar to his own that he will be comprehended instantly, and will not be asked, for instance, "Much *what*?" The traditional Englishman's reputation for taciturnity stems from his tendency to remain within his own social group, where there isn't much to say because everyone knows the same things and feels the same way about them.

In America, unlike in Britain, there really is such a thing as journalese. That is, there are words that are used in newsprint and heard on newscasts and nowhere else, words such as *gridiron*, *leatherneck*, and *parley*.

American speech continues to be influenced by the overheated language of much of the media, which is designed to attach an impression of exciting activity to passive, if sometimes significant, events. Someone *fires off* a letter, *hits* a bank for a loan, and *grabs* some lunch. The fraudulent nature of this kind of language was brought home to me when I heard someone say he was going to "grab some sleep."

Yet curiously, really violent activity is often described in bland, antiseptic tones that serve to disguise the reality. During the Vietnam War, the US military bureaucracy was well known for the terms it used to disguise the brutal business of war, such as *ordnance expended* for bombs dropped. Very recently a BBC report by Panorama on weapons in space showed a Pentagon official talking about an American satellite that could *negate by impact* a Soviet satellite, meaning that it could destroy it by crashing into it.

The American language has less regard than the British for grammatical form, and will bulldoze its way across its distinctions rather than steer a path between them. It will casually use one form of word for another, turning nouns into verbs, as with *author*, *fund*, and *host* (*scalp*, which was originally only a noun, is an early example of this), and vice versa. This practice is spreading to Britain also. Even the quality newspapers reporting the conflict in Northern Ireland have used the noun *shoot out* and the verb *gun down*.

However, this bluntness is not seen in the heart of the language, the relation of words to meaning. American speech is not more direct and forthright than British. If anything, it tends to flabbiness, loading sentences with circumlocutions and abstractions, and inflating some words so that they lose strength and substance, words like *great* and *disaster*. A Briton may be misled by this, thinking that if an American responds to a suggestion with *Terrific!* this signifies rapturous enthusiasm, whereas it is only polite assent.

In this connection, it is interesting to note that when, some years ago Professor Alan Ross, the British linguist, published a celebrated study of upper-class and non-upper-class language in Britain, classifying words and phrases as U (for upper-class) and *non-U*, most Americans writing about it missed the point entirely. They assumed it was the upper crust who would use the genteel, pussy-footing term, whereas in almost every instance it was the non-U term that is more genteel and circumlocutory, the U more direct—a product of the U person's natural confidence.

I remember one time when I was a reporter in the London bureau of the Associated Press, coming back to the office with a story about an important sale of paintings, in which I quoted a baronet as saying that someone had "plonked down a hundred thousand smackers." The news editor was one of those Americans who still see and portray England as a place where doddering dukes grope their way through pea soup fogs dratting the fact that they've dropped their blasted monocles. He would not allow the phrase in the story because he said Americans would not recognize a member of the British aristocracy talking like that. I wasted a good deal of time trying to persuade him, not just that this was what the man said, but that this was just the sort of thing that he would say.

Yet sometimes, it is the American language that is the more muscular of the two, for instance, in the hands of some of the finest American prose stylists, such as Hemingway and J. D. Salinger, and in some of the best American magazine journalism. In different ways, either one or the other may be the more robust, elegant, precise or colorful.

The title of this book deserves a note of explanation. Some people will object that there is no such thing as the British language, that Britons speak English. It is true that English is the language that, along with its users, conquered Welsh and the Gaelic of Scotland, and that it is certainly not in its origins a Scottish or Welsh language. But to call this an English/American language guide would imply that Americans do not speak English. So *British* is used here to mean the predominant language spoken in the British Isles, as distinct from that spoken in other parts of the English-speaking world.

A few more words about what is and is not found here. Meanings that are common to the two languages are not necessarily included, even where the word is in here with another meaning. For instance, in the British/American section, the word *chemist* is defined as a druggist. It is not explained that the word in Britain also means a scientist whose field is chemistry, since it means that in America also. Occasionally, the common meaning is included where it might cause confusion otherwise. The sole criterion is what is useful.

Sporting terms are not included except where they are used outside the context of the game. If an American goes to a cricket match, he expects to hear unfamiliar words that he would not hear anywhere else. However, he may be talking to an Englishman about anything at all and hear that someone is *on a sticky wicket*. Just as, if the Englishman has fallen among Americans, he might hear it said that someone has *two strikes against him*. So the cricket term *wicket* is defined, and the baseball term *strike*. In other areas, specialized terms are included and explained if the non-specialist is likely to encounter them, shopping for the household, in business, or in a newspaper's political or financial columns, for instance.

One other class of words deserves mention, though not included in the dictionary. There are some words that are in the language of both countries, but that seem to come with the accent of only one. For instance, an American would be unlikely to use the word *bottom*, as in "He fell on his bottom," or *crafty* as in "That was a crafty move." Similarly, there are words which, although perfectly acceptable in Britain, sound more natural on American lips, such as *liquor* and *vacation*.

Words are not included that are particular to only one part of the country (an exception is made with some cockney terms, which are heard outside the boundaries of London, and are in any case more likely to be encountered by Americans than other regional terms). In America, the rural South has a whole vocabulary of its own, and young Southern Californians have a special language, that changes every six months. There is no attempt to include here archaic words, however colorful or philologically interesting. Differences in spelling are not included, what the pseudonymous American poet Firth, in his poem *Orthography*, calls "The lure of the East when Kipling spells 'pyjamas'."

I have tried to make this language guide comprehensive, but not exhaustive.

American/British

A

abolitionist, *n* – an anti-slavery campaigner in pre-Civil War America; the anti-slavery movement.

AC/DC, *adj* (abbr) – 1. attachable to either alternating or direct current. 2. bisexual.

Acapulco gold, *n* – a common, Mexican-grown variety of marijuana.

access television, *n* – not quite what it is in Britain, but a television programme made by a station affiliated to a network but independently of the network.

adjuster, *n* – (in insurance) an assessor.

administration, *n* – a cabinet and other officials appointed by the President. One speaks of 'the Reagan Administration' as one would 'the Thatcher Government', although it includes more people. On the difference between British and American terminology, F.J. Goodnow, in his Book *Politics and Administration*, offers this explanation: 'The one, through its control of Parliament, makes as well as administers laws; the other merely administers laws made by Congress.'

adobe, *n* – a sun-dried brick made of earth or clay. Adobe houses are common in the Southwest. This is a Spanish word that has crossed the Rio Grande. Pronounced 'a-doe-bee'.

aerosol bomb, *n* – an insecticide spray.

affair, *n* – this also means a party or other planned social occasion. Thus, a catering firm advertising in the *New York Post*, 18 Feb, 1982: 'For any kind of affair. You can have it in your own living room.'

AFL/CIO, *n* (abbr) – the American Federation of Labor/Congress of Industrial Organizations, the national trade union body. It was formed by the merger of these two separate organizations in 1955, the AFL the older, and the CIO, formed during the New Deal, and more militant.

air, *n* – to give someone the air means to turn one's back on him or her. Also used sometimes about a thing, meaning to give it up.

air cushion vehicle, *n* – hovercraft. Sometimes abbreviated to **ACV**.

aisle, *n* – a gangway in a church, store or any other building; e.g. 'the British fashion of having railway compartments instead of an undivided car with a nice long aisle' – from *Dodsworth* by Sinclair Lewis.

à la mode, *adj* – with ice cream.

alderman, *n* – a local official elected separately from councillors. In most localities in America, aldermen form a separate legislative body.

alfalfa, *n* – a leafy plant related to the bean grown widely in the United States and used as fodder. The approximate British equivalent is lucerne.

Alger, *prop n* – see Horatio Alger.

all-American, *adj* – in the top class in a particular sport. In some sports, newspapers will choose an imaginary 'all-American' team composed of the best players.

all-fired, *adv* (col) – tremendously, extremely. An old-fashioned, rural-sounding term.

alligator pear, *n* – avocado.

alma mater, *n* – one's old school or university.

alumnus, *n* – a graduate of a school or university. The Latin endings are preserved, so that the feminine is **alumna,** and the plural **alumni** and **alumnae.**

ambrosia, *n* – a dessert of fresh orange, bananas, coconut and other fruits.

ambulance-chaser, *n* (col) – a lawyer who rustles up business in unethical ways. Supposedly, he chases ambulances in order to persuade the victim of an accident to sue someone.

American Legion, *prop n* – the largest ex-servicemen's organization, nationalistic in its politics.

American plan, *n* – a hotel rate including meals.

Amtrak, *prop n* – the nationally-owned National Railroad Passenger Corporation, which operates some rail services between major cities.

Angeleno, *n* – a citizen of Los Angeles.

angel food cake, *n* – a light, fluffy, plain cake.

Annapolis, *prop n* – the location of the US Naval Academy, and in common speech the Academy itself; the equivalent of Dartmouth.

annie oakley, *n* (col) – a free ticket to an event. Named after the famous markswoman because these tickets sometimes have a hole punched in them, like a bullet hole.

ante, *n* – the stake in a wager. The term comes from poker. To **ante up** means to put down one's stake. **penny-ante** means cheap, small-time.

ante-bellum, *adj* – pre-American Civil War. One speaks of a Southern ante-bellum mansion.

antenna, *n* – aerial.

antsy, *adj* (col) – jittery. A shortened version of 'ants in his pants'.

apartment, *n* – flat. An **apartment house** is a block of flats.

apartment hotel, *n* – a block of service flats.

ape, *adj* (col) – to **go ape** means to go wild with excitement.

appaloosa, *n* – a hardy breed of horse developed in the American West, distinguished by its mottled colouring.

apple butter, *n* – a spiced apple sauce served as a condiment.

applejack, *n* – a strong, home-brewed liquor distilled from fermented cider.

apple pie order, *adj* (col) – ship-shape, in good order.

apple polisher, *n* – a toady. The term comes from the custom in rural America of bringing teacher an apple as a present to win her favour.

apple sauce, *n* (col) – flattery, usually false.

area code, *n* – dialling code.

armory, *n* – drill hall.

ascot, *n* – a broad scarf worn instead of a tie.

ash can, *n* – dustbin.

ass, *n* (col) – arse. A piece of ass is a common male phrase for a sexy or available girl.

assembly, *n* – in most states, the lower house of the state legislature.

assignment, *n* – homework. A teacher will say, 'Have you done your assignment?'

attorney, *n* – lawyer. Both words are used equally.

audit, *v* – at university, to sit in on a course without the intention of taking the final exam, or getting an academic credit for it.

automat, *n* – a restaurant where food and drink are taken from coin-in-slot machines.

AWOL, *adj* – an acronym for 'absent without leave', originally a service term.

B

Babbit, *n* – a smug, narrow-minded, Philistine middle-class American. From the Sinclair Lewis novel of this name, which portrayed this kind of person. Also **Babbitry.**

baby carrier, *n* – carry cot.

backlog, *n* – this stands for the same thing in Britain and America but has a different meaning. In America, it means a comfortable reserve; an American businessman who says he has a backlog of orders is likely to say it in a tone of self-satisfaction. The word comes from the old log-fire days, and originally meant a log kept in the back of the fire as reserve fuel.

back-up lights, *n* – the reversing lights on a car.

bad, *adj* (col) – very good. Used mostly among young people, it is a black slang word that has recently emerged. Like many minority group terms, this disguises its true meaning from outsiders.

bad-mouth, *v* (col) – to disparage, speak badly of.

bad news, *n* (col) – something that is disagreeable, and spells trouble, as in 'He's bad news. Always has been.'

bag, *n* (col) – 1. one's thing, occupation or preoccupation.

2. to **tie on a bag** means to go on a drinking spree.

bag job, *n* – a burglary by police or agents of a government department, usually to find evidence. The term became known during the Watergate events.

bag-man, *n* – a collector for a crooked organization.

bags, *n* – suitcases.

ball, *n* – baseball. Also **ball park, ball player,** etc.

ball, *v* (col) – to have sexual intercourse.

ballsy, *adj* (col) – gutsy, tough.

ballyhoo, *v* – to publicize with inflated praise.

baloney, *n* – a large, slightly seasoned Italian sausage, sold in delicatessens and popular as a sandwich filler. The word is an aberrant version of Bologna, for Bologna sausage. Used colloquially, it means nonsense, e.g. 'That's a lot of baloney!' is a common dismissive phrase.

banana oil, *n* – soft soap, false flattery. Rare nowadays.

bananas, *adj* (col) – crazy.

Band-Aid, *prop n* – plaster to put on a wound, a trade name that has become a generic term. It is sometimes used metaphorically, for a patch-up job.

bang, *v* (col) – to screw, have sexual intercourse with.

bangs, *n* – hair in a fringe.

bankroll, *n* and *v* – a sum of money. As a verb, it means to put up a sum of money for some purpose; e.g. 'Old debts were paid, dependents bankrolled, and h.q. funded.' – from *The Secret Army: A History of the I.R.A.* by Professor Bowyer Bell.

barbie doll, *n* – originally a trade name for a pretty plastic doll, it now means a girl who seems to be just that.

barf, *v* – to vomit.

barfly, *n* – someone who hangs around bars.

barkeep, *n* – a bartender.

barnstorm, *v* – to travel with a show or theatrical troupe. The term comes from the tradition of travelling players who used to perform in barns.

barrel, *v* – to travel very fast, e.g. 'He was barrelling along the freeway at a cool 90 an hour.'

baseboard, *n* – skirting board.

bash, *n* – party.

bassinet, *n* – an infant's cot made of wickerwork or similar material with a hood at one end.

bass wood, *n* – the wood of any tree of the linden family.

bat, *n* – a bender.

bathe, *v* – to bath. It doesn't mean to swim, though Americans speak of a bathing suit.

bathrobe, *n* – dressing gown.

bathroom, *n* – in America, this nearly always includes a toilet; hence, the word is often a polite synonym for a toilet. If an American visitor asks for the bathroom, he may want the toilet.

battenboard, *n* – perforated hardboard.

batter, *n* – the man wielding the bat in baseball.

bawl, *v* (col) – cry, weep.

bawl out, *v* (col) – to reprimand harshly.

Bay Area, *prop n* – the San Francisco bay area.

bay window, *n* – a bulging stomach.

bayou, *n* – a marshy, sluggish stretch of water, tributary of a river. Characteristic of much of Louisiana, where the word comes from, dating back to the time when the area was colonized by France.

bazooka, *n* – a crude, home-made musical instrument constructed out of a tube and tissue paper, invented and named by the comedian George Burns. The rocket-launcher was so named because it looks like one.

bazoom, *n* (col) – breasts. A comic distortion of 'bosom'.

BB gun, *n* – an air gun. **BB pellets** are the pellets fired by the gun.

bean, *v* (col) – to hit someone on the head, but it is light-hearted and implies no serious injury. For a long time it meant only to hit somebody on the head with the ball in a baseball game, presumably by accident.

beanie, *n* – a small brimless cap, worn by youngsters.

beans, *n* (col) – a small amount, as in 'He knows beans about it,' or sometimes 'He doesn't know beans about it.'

beast, *n* (col) – an unattractive girl. An aggressive, insulting term.

beaver, *n* (col) – the female pudenda.

bee, *n* – a gathering to perform some task, either in cooperation or in competition. A **spelling bee** in school is a contest, a **knitting bee** is a joint venture to provide a new mother with a set of baby clothes. As a neighbourly cooperative effort, it has Colonial and frontier associations. Thomas Pyle, in *Words and Ways of American English*, tells of an eighteenth century Englishman being puzzled by a sentence in a letter from an American cousin: 'The cellar of our new house was dug by a bee in a single day.'

beet, *n* – beetroot.

bell boy, *n* – page boy or porter. A colloquial version is **bellhop**.

belly-flop or **belly-whop,** *n* – to ride downhill on a sled on the stomach.

beltway, *n* – ringroad.

bench, *v* – to put or take someone out of action or out of the game. The term comes from American football, where a player who is pulled off the field is sent to 'sit on the bench', or 'benched'.

Benedict Arnold, *prop n* – one of George Washington's lieutenants in the American War of Independence, who went over to the British side; hence, another term for a traitor.

betty, *n* – a pudding open at the bottom, identified by its filler, e.g. **apple betty, plum betty**.

b-girl, *n* – a bar girl, equivalent to a nightclub hostess in Britain.

Bible Belt, *prop n* – the area where the rural districts are characterized by narrow-mindedness and old-time religion, covering parts of Arkansas, Tennessee and Missouri. Dated, as is the phenomenon.

Big Apple, *prop n* (col) – New York City.

big-foot, *n* – a large, hairy, man-like creature, reputed to have been seen in the woods of the Pacific Northwest. America's answer to the abominable snowman.

bill, *n* – a money note, as a dollar bill.

billboard, *n* – 1. hoarding. 2. in radio, an announcement of what is to come.

billfold, *n* – wallet.

Bircher, *n* – member of the ultra-nationalist John Birch Society; he was an American missionary in China killed by the Communists.

billion, *n* – 1,000 million. The traditional British billion is 1,000 times as much, but the American usage has gained wide currency in Britain in recent years.

billy, *n* – truncheon.

bimbo, *n* (col) – a girl, a disrespectful term.

bird dog, *n* – gun dog.

biscuit, *n* – similar to a scone.

bitch, *v* (col) – to complain. Though the word is used widely in its other, pejorative sense, both as a noun and adjectively ('bitchy'), this word in all its other uses is unisex. It carries no feminine connotation, and is used widely, for instance, in the services. **bitch up** means to foul up or make a mess of a situation.

bitch, *n* (col) – something disagreeable, e.g. 'This job is a bitch.'

bite, *n* (col) – to put the bite on someone means to ask them for money.

bits, *n* (col) – 12½ cents. Used only in the plural, in even multiples. Two bits is 25 cents, four bits is 50 cents, and so on. A high school cheer goes: 'Two bits, four bits, six bits, a dollar! Everyone for Waukegan stand up and holler!'

black, *n* and *adj* – Negro. 'Black' is preferred among the modern-minded to 'Negro' or 'coloured'.

black-eyed Susan, *n* – a North American wild flower of genus *Rudbeckia* with dark brown centre and yellowish petals.

blackjack, *n* – a club or cosh.

blacktop, *n* – a bituminous metal used for surfacing roads.

blank, *n* – certain forms. Americans speak of a telegraph blank.

blast, *n* (col) – a party. A young people's word.

bleachers, *n* – the cheap, uncovered stand in a sports stadium.

blitzed, *adj* – drunk.

blinders, *n* – blinkers on a horse.

blind-side, *v* – to catch someone unawares by coming up out of their line of vision. 'In Iran, the CIA was blind-sided by Khomeini's rebellion.' – *Newsweek*, 10 October 1983.

block, *n* – a city block bounded by streets on all four sides, or a street one block long. Distance in American cities is often measured in blocks.

block-busting, *v part* – moving a lower-class family or several families into a block so that the other residents begin to move out, and the character and rental values change.

blooper, *n* (col) – mistake, boob.

blotter, *n* – an official record of the events of the day, particularly at a police station.

blow, *v* (col) – 1. get out, scram. 2. wreck, destroy, dissipate, usually in the abstract, as in 'That blew all my plans', or 'He blew his cool.'

blowhard, *n* (col) – a loudmouth, a person who talks big about himself.

blow-out, *n* – 1. a puncture. 2. (col) an extravagant party.

blow out, *v* (col) – to astound, flabbergast, as in 'That blew me out!'

blueberry, *n* – an edible North American berry, resembling a red berry only blue in colour.

bluebook, *n* – a book listing the names of socially prominent families.

blue chip, *adj* – sound (of a share) with low risk and unspectacular returns.

blue collar, *adj* – pertaining to industrial workers, as distinct from white collar.

Blue Cross, Blue Shield, *n* – the largest private American health insurance organizations.

bluegrass, *n* – a kind of grass that has a blueish tinge. The Bluegrass State is Kentucky. Also, bluegrass now means a kind of country music stemming from Kentucky played without amplifiers.

bluejacket, *n* – a sailor in the US Navy.

blue laws, *n* – puritanical laws relating, for instance, to drink, Sunday entertainment and sex in the media. A **bluenose** is someone intent on enforcing these.

blue point, *n* – the commonest kind of oyster served in the Northeast, much more common than oysters in Britain, caught around Blue Point, Long Island.

BMOC, *n* – **big man on campus,** an undergraduate who is a social leader.

Board of Trade, *prop n* – a local businessmen's organization. It has no official standing.

boardwalk, *n* – a wooden promenade on the ground or sometimes above it, as along a seafront.

bobby pin, *n* – a hair grip.

bobby sox, *n* – 1. woollen ankle-length socks, usually brightly coloured, worn by youngsters of both sexes. The term dates from the 1940s when they were fashionable, and when certain kinds of teenagers were called 'bobby-soxers'. 2. pertaining to girls' baseball, as in 'bobby-sox league'.

bobcat, *n* – an American lynx.

bock beer, *n* – a sweet, dark, German-style beer.

bodacious, *adj* (col) – extraordinary, outrageous, extreme. It is mock-rural, and comes from a comic strip about backwoods folks called *Snuffy Smith*.

boffo or **boffola,** *adj* – smasheroo, a showbiz term indicating a resounding impact.

bohunk, *n* – an immigrant from Central or Eastern Europe, an unpleasant term. It is a combination of Bohemian and **hunkie** or Hungarian.

boiled shirt, *n* – a stiff evening shirt.

boilerplate, *n* – material in a newspaper that is usable as space-filler and is dispensable.

bollix up, *v* (col) – to foul up.

boll weevil, *n* – a beetle of the American South which attacks the cotton plant.

bomb, *v* (col) – to fail, to flop; used mostly in the theatre. The word has the opposite meaning to the same word used similarly in Britain. See BOMB in the British/American section. Hence the double meaning in the title of Joseph Heller's play about a touring theatrical company with a play about a bombing mission which is and is not real, *We Bombed In New Haven.*

bond, *n* – an insurance policy guaranteeing compensation to an employer for loss through an employee's unauthorized or illegal acts.

bonds, *n* – stock.

bondsman, *n* – someone whose occupation is standing surety for people arrested and released on bail, at a high interest rate.

boner, *n* – gaffe, resounding mistake.

bone-on, *n* (col) – erection.

boo-boo, *n* (col) – a mistake, a boob.

boob tube, *n* (col) – television.

booby hatch, *n* (col) – mental home. 'You are a booby and you will be put in a booby hatch,' the Thurberish wife tells her husband in James Thurber's *The Unicorn in the Garden.*

boodle, *n* (col) – bribe money. From the Dutch *boedel*.

boondocks, *n* – the backwoods, a remote rural area. Also sometimes **boonies**.

boondoggle, *n* (col) – useless time-wasting activity.

booster, *n* – a professional talker-up, singing the praises of something.

boot camp, *n* – US Marine Corps training camp.

boozer, *n* (col) – a drinker; never a bar.

boss, *adj* (col) – great, wonderful. A word from black slang that has emerged recently into the wider world.

Boston Brahmin, *n* – one of the old Bostonian Anglo-Saxon aristocracy.

Boston cream pie, *n* – a round cake with a cream or custard filling.

bouncer, *n* – a chucker-out.

bourbon, *n* – whisky distilled from maize. Its original home was Bourbon County, Kentucky. Pronounced as 'burrbon'.

Bowery, *prop n* – a street in lower New York City, the centre of skid row.

box car, *n* – a goods wagon on a train.

box score, *n* – a detailed tabulation of results in a baseball game.

braids, *n* – plaits.

brainstorm, *v* (col) – to get together and bounce ideas off one another, hoping to produce something.

brakeman, *n* – a guard on a train.

branch water, *n* – water from a fast-flowing branch of a river

or stream which is therefore cleaner and purer than tap water. Bourbon was traditionally drunk with branch water in the old South, but today 'bourbon and branch water', a common phrase, is a cute way of saying simply bourbon with water in it.

brickbat, *n* – a part of a brick, particularly when used as a missile.

broad, *n* (col) – woman.

broad jump, *n* – long jump.

broiler, *n* – like a grill, only deeper.

Bronx cheer, *n* – a raspberry (the Bronx is a part of New York City).

Brooks Brothers, *prop n* – in the style of this men's clothing shop in New York, which provides smart but conservative tailoring, typically for business executives.

brownie, *n* – a small, heavy, chocolate-flavoured cake, a children's favourite.

Brownie points, *n* – kudos, credit that could lead to advancement. The term is a little ironic since it is taken from the Brownies, the junior Girl Guides (the Girl Scouts in America). 'Nobody got Brownie points for caring about nuclear waste. The Atomic Energy Commission neglected the problem.' – Carroll Wilson, former General Manager of the AEC in an article.

brown-nose, *n* – toady. Its literal meaning is scatalogical.

brownstone, *n* – a reddish-brown sandstone much used in urban building, particularly by prosperous people in the early years of this century; **brown-stone house** is a common description for such a house, now often broken up into flats or bed-sitting rooms.

brunch, *n* – a mid-morning meal (the word is a combination of 'breakfast' and 'lunch') eaten usually on weekends, often as a social occasion.

BTO, (abbr, col) – big time operator.

buck, *n* (col) – a dollar.

buck, *v* (col) – to oppose a prevailing trend or force, as to 'buck the system'.

buckaroo, *n* – cowboy. A Western term. A corruption of the Spanish word *vaquero*.

buckboard, *n* – a horse-drawn cart with a raised seat for driver and passenger.

bucket shop, *n* – a crooked stocks-and-shares brokerage firm.

buckeye, *n* – horse chestnut. The **Buckeye State** is Ohio.

buck for, *v* – to go for, aim at. 'The Democratic Party task forces are staffed by activists bucking for policy-making jobs.' – columnist Stephen S. Rosenfeld, *International Herald Tribune*, 24 May 1976.

bucksaw, *n* – a two-handled wooden saw.

buddy, *n* (col) – a friend, a pal. It is a little small townish, old-fashioned now. A favourite song of the 1920s went: 'I don't want a girl, I want a buddy/Cos buddies never make you cry.' (In that innocent age, this sentiment had no sexual overtones.) It is also used as a term of address, menacingly more often than affectionately, as in 'Now look here, buddy . . .'

buffalo, *v* (col) – to bulldoze or pressure someone into doing something.

bug, *v* – annoy, irritate, as in 'What bugs me is that . . .'

bug, *n* (col) – flaw, difficulty, usually used in the plural, and in a technological context, e.g. 'It'll take a week to iron the bugs out of this project.' This is one of several words that Dr David Dalby, the London University philologist, has shown to have come into America from West African languages, having been brought over by slaves. (Others are 'dig', 'jitters' and – this is more controversial, though Dr Dalby argues the case persuasively – 'Okay'.)

buggy, *n* – a small, four-wheeled horse-drawn carriage.

building and loan association, *n* – something like a building society.

bull, *n* (col) – nonsense; an abbreviation of 'bull-shit'.

bullhorn, *n* – megaphone.

bull pen, *n* (col) – any temporary confinement area, for instance, a prison cell where people are held pending a court appearance. In baseball, it means the enclosed area on the field where players can warm up and wait to go in to play.

bull session, *n* (col) – a period of informal talk.

bum, *n* – 1. a tramp. This is one of those words from America that has now established more than a toe-hold in Britain and will probably be widely accepted soon with this meaning, rather than the anatomical one. 2. a general term of abuse, meaning just a no-good person.

bum, *adj* – bad, inferior.

bum, *v* – cadge, as in 'Can I bum a cigarette off you?' To **bum around** is to knock around idly.

bummer, *n* – something that is no good, a flop.

bumper car, *n* – dodgem car.

bumps and grinds, *n* – the gyrations of a striptease dancer.

bum's rush, *n* – the action of throwing someone out by the scruff of his neck and the seat of his trousers.

bunco game, *n* – a crooked card game.

bunny, *n* (col) – a dolly bird. The term comes from the Playboy bunnies.

bunt, *v* – to tap a ball very lightly with a bat; a baseball term.

bureau, *n* – chest of drawers.

burlap, *n* – a coarse canvas, used for covering or sacks.

burner, *n* – hob on a stove. To put (something) **on the back burner** means to set it aside for a while.

burro, *n* – donkey, a Mexican word.

bus, *v* – to take children by bus to a racially mixed school in another area, in order to ensure racially integrated schooling.

bus boy, *n* – commis waiter.

bushel, *n* – 2,150 cubic inches, instead of 2,219 cubic inches as in a British bushel.

bush league, *n* – the minor league in baseball. Often used metaphorically: 'He was only in the bush league in those days' means that he was only small fry compared with his present status.

bushwah, *n* (col) – nonsense.

bushwhack, *n* – 1. to travel through rough, bushy country. 2. to ambush in bushy countryside.

bushwhacker, *n* – during the Civil War, a Confederate guerrilla. Often used now for any guerrilla.

buss, *n* and *v* (col) – kiss. This is getting old-fashioned, and now sounds rather quaint.

bust, 1. *n* and *v* – arrest. 2. a total failure, or, as a verb, to fail. 3. party.

butt, *n* (col) – 1. cigarette. 2. bottom, arse.

butter-and-eggs-man, *n* – a man out spending in a restaurant or night club. Also a well known Louis Armstrong song.

button-down, *adj* – conventional and conservative in style, after button-down shirt collars in which the corners of the lapels are buttoned down, an American garment that never took on among button-down people in Britain.

buzz, *n* (col) – 1. a telephone call, as in 'I'll give you a buzz.' 2. A slight high induced by drink or drugs.

BVDs, *n* – a trade name for a brand of men's underwear that was so popular in the West for a while that the term now means men's underwear in general.

BYO, *v* – bring your own. You might find this on an invitation to a party, in which case it is a bottle party.

C

cabana, *n* – beach hut.

caboose, *n* – the last wagon on a goods train.

caddy, *n* – shopping trolley.

Caesar salad, *n* – a salad made with raw egg and cheese.

Cajun, *n* – referring to one of a group of people in rural Louisiana who are descended from the French settlers who migrated there from Nova Scotia ('Cajun' is a corruption of 'Arcadian') and have retained a trace of their patois.

cakewalk, *n* – a prancing walk to music. Originally, this was a feature of black parties in the South, with a prize of a cake going to the best.

calaboose, *n* – a local jail. Mostly Western.

call-in, *n* – phone-in. Both terms are used.

can, *n* – 1. a tin, as in 'a can of soup' or 'canned fruit'. 2. (col) toilet. 3. (col) arse, e.g. 'He fell on his can.'

can, *v* (col) – 1. to close off or shut off. 'Can that talk!' means 'stop talking like that!' In the passive sense, it means sacked, dismissed from employment. 2. to preserve food. A family 'canning peaches' may be putting them in bottles.

candy, or candies, *n* – sweets.

candy-assed, *adj* (col) – timid, sissyish.

Canuck, *n* (col) – a Canadian, particularly French-Canadian.

canvasser, *n* – a scrutineer of votes; sometimes also the meaning in Britain, a canvasser for a political party.

Capitol Hill, *prop n* – the hill in Washington D.C. on which the Capitol, the building of Congress, is located. Used in political discussion, it is a synonym for Congress. Sometimes shortened to the Hill.

capri pants, *n* – women's tight-fitting trousers.

captain, *n* – the leader of a group, used in a number of ways it would not be in Britain: for instance, in a hotel, the chief of the bell boys (or porters, as they would be in Britain) is the bell captain.

car, *n* – carriage, as in railroad car and pullman car.

carfare, *n* – money for bus or tube fare. It used to mean streetcar (tram) fare.

car hop, *n* – a waiter or waitress at a drive-in restaurant who serves customers in their cars. Also, the man at a parking lot who parks the cars.

carousel, *n* – merry-go-round.

carpet bagger, *n* – a Northerner who went to the South in the aftermath of the Civil War to exploit for profit the situation of defeat and social and economic disintegration. By extension, anyone who sets out to exploit such a situation.

carry-all, *n* – a car similar to an estate car, but higher, usually on a lorry chassis. *Webster's* says it comes from the French *carriole* meaning a light carriage.

carry-out, *v part* – 'take-away'. as in a **carry-out counter** in some eating places.

casket, *n* – in general use, a coffin. It means something else only if specified, e.g. jewel casket.

cater-corner, *n* – in a diagonal or oblique position. Also **catty-corner**. This is apparently adopted from the sound of the French phrase *à quatre coin*.

cat-house, *n* (col) – brothel.

catsup, *n* – ketchup.

caucus, *n* – this has a more specific meaning than in Britain, meaning a small group of a political gathering that meets to take a decision. The word came to Britain from America, and is thought to stem from an Algonquin Indian word.

caucus, *v* – to go into caucus.

centennial, *n* – centenary.

central time, *n* – one of the four standard time zones in the United States, six hours behind GMT.

certified check, *n* – a cheque which contains a certification from the bank that the money is there and has been set aside for payment.

certified letter, *n* – a letter that is certified by a notary as proof of its authorship. The certification does not relate to the contents.

chaparral, *n* – the thick scrub country of Southwest USA, mainly evergreen oaks.

chaps, *n* – the leather leggings worn in the West for riding and ranch work.

chap-stick, *n* – lip-salve.

charge nurse, *n* – ward sister.

Charlie, *prop n* (col) – the Vietcong, an abbreviation of Victor Charlie.

charlie horse, *n* – a stiffness in the leg, or sprain, or a blow that causes it.

charter member, *n* – founder member.

chaser, *n* – a long drink to soothe the throat after drinking spirits, e.g. 'We were drinking rye with ginger ale chasers,' or, from *Archy & Mehitabel* by Don Marquis: 'If you will drink hair restorer, follow every dram with some good depilatory as a chaser.'

chattel mortgage, *n* – a mortgage on moveable goods.

check, *n* – a bill for food or drink. It also has the meaning of cheque.

checkers, *n* – draughts.

checking account, *n* – current account at a bank.

check off, *v* – tick off.

check-out counter, *n* – the cash desk at a supermarket.

checkroom, *n* – left luggage office.

cheesecloth, *n* – muslin.

cheezit, *v* (col) – watch out! 'Cheezit the cops!' is a comic book cliché.

chef's salad, *n* – a meal-sized

salad which includes strips of meat, cheese and hard-boiled egg.

cherry, *n* (col) – hymen. The last cartoon in the American book *Fractured French* shows a bride leaving a church and waving over her shoulder with the caption 'Adieu chérie'.

cherrystone clam, *n* – a medium-sized clam.

chew out, *v* (col) – to tell off, reprimand severely.

Chicano, *n* – a Mexican-American.

chicken, *adj* (col) – cowardly. To **chicken out** is to back out through cowardice.

chicken à la king, *n* – chicken diced and creamed with pimento or green pepper.

chicory, *n* – the ground root of the plant sometimes used to adulterate coffee. The vegetable itself is called **endive**.

Chief Executive, *prop n* – the President of the United States.

chiffon, *n* – a dessert with a light, frothy texture, made with egg whites and flavouring.

chinch, *n* – a small insect, particularly a bed bug.

Chinook, *prop n* – a warm wind in the Western states, called for some reason after the Chinook Indian tribes of the Northwest. A Chinook is also a large helicopter flown by the US Air Force.

chipped beef, *n* – flaked, dried beef.

chipper, *adj* – cheery and lively.

chips, *n* – potato crisps. Chips are **French fried potatoes**.

chisel, *v* (col) – to cheat.

chocolate chips, *n* – specks of chocolate embedded in a dessert, sometimes called polka dots in Britain.

chorine, *n* – chorus girl.

chowder, *n* – thick fish soup or stew, often made with pork and bacon added.

chuck steak, *n* – slices of steak from the forequarters of the animal.

chuck up, *v* – to vomit.

chuck wagon, *n* – in the West, a waggon carrying provisions for cowboys or farm hands.

chutzpah, *n* (col) – colossal nerve. A Yiddish word. See entry for STAG. The 'ch' is pronounced as a throaty 'h'.

cigar store, *n* – tobacconist's shop.

cinch, *n* (col) – something easy to accomplish, a push-over, a sure thing.

city editor, *n* – a newspaper editor in charge of local news. It has nothing to do with finance.

cladding, *n* – much more limited than the term in Britain, this means only a metal covering on metal.

clapboard, *n* – overlapping planks.

clerk or **sales clerk**, *n* – shop assistant. Pronounced 'clurk'.

clipping, *n* – a cutting from a newspaper or magazine, or, among gardeners, from a plant.

cloakroom, *n* – in Congress, a meeting place for gossip and informal exchanges. In a political context, **cloakroom talk** is the equivalent of 'lobby talk'.

closet, *n* – cupboard. Like a number of American words, this was current in Britain two centuries ago but is no longer used as a noun. A relic is WC for water closet.

closet, *adj* (col) – secret, unacknowledged. Until recently, this was used only in the term **closet queen**, meaning a secret homosexual, but now it is applied more widely. A Pentagon planner has been described as a 'closet dove'.

clothes pin, *n* – clothes peg.

cloture, *n* – a term used in political assemblies for winding up a session or debate.

clout, *n* – influence, weight. Supreme Court Justice William O. Douglas referred in a historic opinion on the death sentence to the danger of 'feeding prejudice against the accused if he is poor and lacking political clout'.

club steak, *n* – a steak cut from the end of the sirloin; the wing rib to a butcher.

clunker, *n* (col) – an old car; a banger, and an equally onomatopoeic word.

coaster, *n* – a small table mat put under a glass when serving drinks.

coat, *n* – it also means jacket.

co-ed, *n* – a girl undergraduate. It derives, obviously, from 'co-educational'.

coffee cake, *n* – not coffee-flavoured, but a fluffy, plainish cake sliced and eaten with morning coffee. Like a larger Danish pastry.

cold duck, *n* – a drink made of mixing red and sparkling wines. The drink and the term come directly from the German. These days you can get cold duck flavoured ice cream.

college, *n* – in common speech, synonymous with university. Strictly speaking, the word refers to an institute of higher education that does not have graduate schools. Thus Yale and Northwestern are universities while Swarthmore and Hamilton are colleges, though their bachelor's degrees have equivalent status. But someone who is studying at any of these will say he is at college.

Colonial, *adj* – pertaining to the first three-quarters of the eighteenth century in America, when Britain ruled the thirteen colonies, or the styles of that period, e.g. 'Colonial-style furniture'.

colorwash, *n* – a coloured distemper.

come-on, *n* (col) – a lure, enticement.

come on to, *v* (col) – to make a pass at someone.

comer, *n* – someone who is up and coming, who is expected to rise to great heights.

comforter, *n* – a soft quilt.

comfort station, *n* – public convenience.

commencement, *n* – the ceremony of graduation from high school or university, so-called because it marks the commencement of a new stage in one's life.

commercial paper, *n* – a promissory note that can be negotiated.

commissary, *n* – a store that supplies food and other goods in a mining camp or military establishment.

common stock. *n* – ordinary shares.

commuter ticket, *n* – season ticket.

Comstock League, *prop n* – an organization famous in the last century for combating zealously sex or salacity in art and literature. Also **Comstockery,** a word introduced into the language by Bernard Shaw, after the society headed by Anthony Comstock had caused his play *Mrs Warren's Profession* to be closed in New York. Shaw wrote: 'Comstockery is the world's standing joke at the expense of the United States.'

concert master, *n* – the leader of an orchestra, usually the first violinist.

concourse, *n* – an open space where people can walk and meet, often with shops, as at a railway station or on the ground floor of some of the large American office buildings.

condominium, *n* – an owner-occupied flat.

cone, *n* – a cornet, as in ice cream cone.

confab, *n* (col) – informal chat.

confectionery sugar, *n* – icing sugar.

Confederacy, *prop n* – the union of Southern States in the American Civil War. **Confederate,** *adj* – applying to the Confederacy, e.g. Confederate troops.

congressman, *n* – though Congress has two houses, this always means a member of the lower house, the House of Representatives (as 'Member of Parliament' always means a member of the lower house, the Commons).

Conservative Jew, *n* – roughly similar to a Reform Jew in Britain in his limited deviation from orthodoxy.

cookie, *n* – a sweet or semi-sweet biscuit.

cookie-pusher, *n* (col) – someone whose principal function is a social one, such as giving cocktail parties. A disparaging term.

cookie sheet, *n* – baking tray.

cook-out, *n* – festive meal cooked out of doors.

coon, *n* – racoon.

copesetic, *adj* (col) – fine, excellent, going smoothly.

cop out, *v* – to evade an obligation. 'A motive occasionally offered for remaining in the ghetto is racial solidarity. Leaving less fortunate brothers behind is copping out.' – from *Soulside* by Ulf Hannery. As a noun it becomes **cop-out.**

copy-reader, *n* – a sub-editor, one who edits copy on a newspaper and writes headlines.

cord, *n* – 1. string, wire or flex. 2. a measure of timber, 128 cubic feet.

corduroy road, *n* – road over marshy ground, made of logs.

cord wood, *n* – wood cut into planks; technically it means into a quantity totalling a cord.

corn, *n* – maize, and no other grain. This was discovered in America, and Britons at first called it 'Indian corn'. Mary Helen Dohan says, in her book about the American language *Our Own Words,* with some perception, that when the early settlers adopted this English word for their vital crop, it was 'the word that was most clearly a linguistic declaration of independence'.

cornball, *n* and *adj* – corny, or something corny.

corn bread, *n* – a bread made of maize meal. Also, **corn cake, corn muffin.**

corncob pipe, *n* – a pipe with a bowl made from a hollowed-out corn cob, a traditional rural accessory. General Douglas MacArthur always sported one.

corn dodger, *n* – corn bread that is baked or fried hard.

corned beef, *n* – salt beef.

corn liquor, *n* – crude spirits produced from maize, usually home-made.

corn pone, *n* – a plain bread made of corn meal, characteristically Southern.

cornstarch, *n* – cornflour.

corporation, *n* – limited company.

cot, *n* – camp bed.

cotillion, *n* – a dance of the quadrille kind, or an elaborate ball.

cottager, *n* – someone owning or renting a holiday house at a resort. 'It has ceased to be fashionable to bathe at Newport. Strangers and servants may do so, but the cottagers have withdrawn their support from the ocean.' – from *Their Pilgrimage* by David Warner, published in 1887, which shows also that weighty Victorian social distinctions were not confined to Britain.

cotton candy, *n* – candy floss.

cottonwood tree, *n* – a tree much like a poplar with cotton-like hairs on the seed.

coulee, *n* – a stream, or sometimes, the dry bed of a creek.

counselor, *n* – 1. lawyer. This is a formal mode of address to a lawyer in some states. 2. someone who takes care of kids at a summer camp, an American urban middle-class institution.

counterman, *n* – a man who serves at a snack bar or lunch counter.

coupé, *n* – a closed two-door car.

coupon-clipper, *n* (col) – someone who lives on an income from stocks and shares.

courtesy car, *n* – a car sent by a hotel without charge to collect guests from an airport or station.

cow-catcher, *n* – a triangular frame on the front of an old locomotive, designed to sweep obstructions out of the way.

cowpea, *n* – a vegetable closer to a bean than a pea, grown mostly for forage.

coyote, *n* – a prairie wolf that inhabits the American West.

CPA, *n* (abbr) – certified public accountant, the equivalent of a chartered accountant.

crab grass, *n* – a weed that grows particularly on lawns.

crack, *n* (col) – vagina. Obscene.

crack up, *v* (col) – to fall about laughing. The verb can be either transitive or intransitive, e.g. 'I just crack up,' or 'That cracks me up.'

cracker, *n* – a poor or uneducated white in the rural South. 'Billy Carter, the incorrigible cracker who still uses the word "nigger" when he's drinking with his friends.' – article in *Playboy*, November 1976.

cracker barrel, *n* – the barrel containing crackers that formed the central point of the general store in an old-fashioned small town, and in folklore, the centre of town conversation and gossip. It is used in expressions like 'cracker barrel philosopher', conjuring up a homely image.

crackerjack, *adj* – excellent, first-rate.

cranberry, *n* – a red berry, used for making a jelly-like sauce; cranberry sauce.

crankcase, *n* – in a car, the housing which encloses the crank shaft, connecting rods and associated parts.

craps, *n* – a popular American gambling game, played with dice. The spelling is changed when it is used in combination, so that one says **crap-game** and **crap-shooting** (playing craps).

crawfish, *n* – crayfish.

crawfish, *v* – to walk sideways, or metaphorically, to hedge.

cream, *v* – to slaughter, either literally, like a regiment in a battle, or figuratively, like a team in a game.

crib, *n* – a cot as well as a crib.

crimp, *n* – a dreary, boring person.

critter, *n* (col) – animal. It is a corruption of 'creature'.

crosswalk, *n* – a pedestrian crossing.

crotch, *n* – crutch, as a part of the anatomy. Both words are American.

crow, *n* – humble pie, in the expression to **eat crow**.

crud, *n* (col) – a piece of filth; a term of abuse, mostly schoolboy.

cruet, *n* – not what it is in Britain, but a bottle for vinegar or sauce.

cruller, *n* – a small fried cake, or else a kind of ring doughnut.

cup, *n* – as a measure, it is 8 oz, as against 10 in Britain.

cupboard, *n* – a kitchen cupboard, a larder. A cupboard in any other room is a **closet**.

curve ball, *n* (col) – a trick or ruse. From the baseball term for a ball thrown by a pitcher that supposedly curves in mid-air.

cut, *n* – a block in printing.

cutesy, *adj* (col) – over-cute, and usually self-consciously so.

D

dad-blamed, *adj* – darned. Mostly rural.

dago red, *n* (col) – cheap red wine. Now used humorously.

dander, *n* (col) – temper, as in 'Don't get your dander up.'

dandy, *adj* – fine, good.

DAR, *n* (abbr) – Daughters of the American Revolution, a patriotic women's society, descendants of Americans of the War of Independence period proud of their descent. 'Nately's mother, a descendant of the New England Thorntons, was a Daughter of the American Revolution. His father was a Son of a Bitch.' – from *Catch 22* by Joseph Heller.

date, *v* – to go out with someone on a date. **double-date,** *n* – on a date with another couple making a foursome. 'I met Jack Kennedy in 1946. We were both war heroes and he had been elected to Congress. We went on a double-date one night and it turned out to be a fair evening for me.' – the opening lines of *An American Dream* by Norman Mailer. **interdate,** *v* – to date someone of another race or religion, a counterpart of 'intermarry'. Thus, a *New York Times* report said recently that on one campus, 'Among the Catholic students, 74 percent interdated frequently.'

datebook, *n* – pocket or desk diary, appointment book. American sensibly distinguishes this from a journal, whereas British uses the same word for both.

davenport, *n* – a large sofa. Davenport, Iowa, used to be the centre of the American furniture industry. The word is slipping out of use.

day bed, *n* – studio couch.

daylight saving time, *n* – summer time when the clocks are put forward an hour.

deacon's bench, *n* – a wooden seat for two, in Colonial style.

deadhead, *adj* – empty, used about a vehicle, e.g. 'The truck carried four tons of concrete to Baltimore, and came back deadhead.'

deadhead, *n* (col) – 1. one who attends a theatre, rides on transport, etc., without paying. 2. someone who is deadly dull.

debark, *v* – disembark.

decal, *n* – a transfer, as used by children, or by manufacturers on car windscreens, etc.

deck, *n* – 1. a pack of cards. 2. (col) floor.

deck shoes, *n* – same as boat

shoes, plimsolls with thick crepe soles.

deed, *v* – to transfer by title deed.

den mother, *n* – a woman who leads a cub scout pack

department store, *n* – a big store.

depot, *n* – station. Both words are used, though 'station' is more big city.

derby, *n* – a bowler hat. It also has the same sporting meaning as in Britain. It is pronounced differently, the first syllable rhyming with 'curb'.

devil's food cake, *n* – a rich, chocolate cake. It may sound like a Satanic concoction, but is harmless, and is served typically with coffee in the evening by genteel old ladies.

diamond, *n* – the central, marked-out area in which baseball is played, actually a square consisting of a home plate and the three bases 90 feet apart.

diamondback, *n* – a domestic American rattlesnake.

diaper, *n* – nappy.

dibs, *n* – claim, as in 'I've got dibs on it.' A juvenile term.

dick, *n* (col) – detective. One of the most famous of W.C. Fields's films is called *The Bank Dick.*

dickey, *n* – a detachable stiff shirt front.

dike, *n* (col) – lesbian.

dime, *n* – a 10-cent piece. This is often taken in Britain to be a slang word, but in fact is the proper name for the coin and is written on its face.

dimmity, *adj* (col) – itsy-bitsy.

diner, *n* – a cheap restaurant, usually with only a counter, often created in the body of an old railway carriage. Also, a restaurant car on a train.

dinette, *n* – a separate eating area that is part of a room.

dingbat, *n* (col) – 1. a stupid or zany person. Mostly a youthful term. 2. a missile, something to throw at someone.

diploma, *n* – usually a certificate of graduation from secondary school, called high school.

dipsy, *n* – a dumb blonde.

dirigible, *n* – zeppelin.

dirt farm, *n* – a humble farm where the going is hard.

dirt road, *n* – an unpaved road.

dirty pool, *n* (col) – unfair behaviour, hitting below the belt.

discombobulate, *v* – to fall to pieces.

dishpan, *n* – washing-up bowl. For years, American soap manufacturers warned the country's womanhood of the miseries of 'dishpan hands'.

disjoint, *v* – in cooking, to joint.

district, *n* – constituency. A congressional district is the equivalent of a parliamentary constituency.

district attorney, *n* – the public prosecutor of a district.

District of Columbia, or **D.C.,** *prop n* – the area in which Washington, the capital city, is situated, run by the Federal government so that no state has sovereignty over it.

ditch, *v* (col) – to play truant.

ditsy, *adj* (col) – stupid.

divided highway, *n* – dual carriageway.

Dixie, *prop n* – the Southern states, Also, a song of that name.

dog, *n* (col) – 1. an insulting term for an unattractive member of the opposite sex, used by and about both sexes. 2. side, as in 'putting on the dog'. A bit old-fashioned.

doggie bag, *n* – a bag provided by a restaurant for carrying scraps of food home for a pet.

doggo, *n* (col) – still and silent, usually for concealment or pretence.

dogie, *n* – a motherless calf. First syllable pronounced to rhyme with 'toe', second with a hard 'g'.

dog-tag, *n* – a military identity disc worn around the neck.

donnybrook, *n* (col) – a row, or riotous gathering. Derived from the Donnybrook Fair in Ireland.

doodie, *n* (col) – turd.

dormitory, *n* – a building that houses a number of students, a hall of residence. See DORMITORY in the British/American section.

double-header, *n* – in baseball, two games played as a single event. The term is often used metaphorically.

doughboy, *n* (col) – an American infantry soldier; a First World War term.

doughnut, *n* – a ring-shaped pastry with a distinctive flavour. It is different entirely from a British doughnut, and not as sweet. It has no filling.

Dow Jones, *prop n* – the standard stock market report, issued in a teleprinter service by Dow Jones and Co. Inc.

downer, *n* – originally a drug users' term meaning a barbiturate, it now means anything or any situation that leaves a person depressed or with depleted energy.

downspout, *n* – drainpipe.

downtown, *n* and *adj* – in the main part of town. But as well as being an area, it also means, in big cities where the streets are numbered, a direction. Thus a person in New York City at 181st Street might say, 'I'm going downtown' if he is going to 42nd Street, or, to someone, 'You walk three blocks downtown,' directing them to a place in 178th Street.

draft, *n* – conscription.

drag, *n* (col) – influence or 'pull'.

drapes, *n* – opaque curtains. Net or lace curtains are always called curtains.

drawers, *n* – underpants.

drive-time, *n* – a term used in radio, meaning the morning or evening period when most potential listeners are driving to or from work.

drop-out, *n* – someone who drops out of school before finishing. Also, as in Britain, someone who drops out of society.

druggist, *n* – a man who dispenses or is licensed to dispense medicines at a drugstore; he is usually the owner or manager.

drugstore, *n* – a shop which dispenses medicines and generally fulfils the functions of a chemist, but sells also a wide variety of other goods, and normally has a counter at which snacks and sometimes meals are served.

drummer, *n* (col) – a commercial traveller.

dry goods, *n* – textiles and fabrics.

dry gulch, *v* (col) – to ambush, waylay. These days the term is unlikely to be encountered outside Western films.

dude, *n* – 1. a dandy, a man who lavishes care on his appearance. 2. one unused to rough work. 3. a man. Like 'cat', this is a black colloquialism that has come into general use.

duded-up, *adj* – all dressed up.

dude ranch, *n* – a place where beginners can ride horses and take part in other supposedly cowboy activities.

dukes, *n* (col) – fists. 'Put up your dukes!' is a schoolboy's challenge to fight.

dumb, *adj* – stupid. It rarely means 'mute'. This distortion of the original meaning occurred very early on in America, and probably stems from the similarity to the Dutch word *dum* which means stupid. (New York was originally a Dutch colony.)

Dun and Bradstreet, *prop n* – the common term for the financial reference book that gives the standing of all major companies.

duplex apartment, *n* – a flat on two floors.

duplex house, *n* – a semi-detached house.

dust bowl, *n* – an area subject to destructive dust storms, particularly the areas around Oklahoma where in the 1930s dust storms ruined many farms and drove people off the land.

Dutch, *adj* (col) – in common speech, this often means German. (It is a corruption of *Deutsch*.) The Pennsylvania Dutch are descendants of German immigrants.

dutch, *n* (col) – to **get in dutch** means to get into trouble. 'I'm in dutch with the teacher' means 'The teacher is angry with me.'

Dutch door, *n* – a half door, divided horizontally.

dutch oven, *n* – a flat iron saucepan with a cover, used for baking.

E

Eastern time or **Eastern standard time** or **EST**, *n* – one of the four standard time zones in the United States, covering the Eastern part of the country. **EDT**, *n* – Eastern daylight time.

eavestrough, *n* – another word for guttering.

editorial, *n* – leading article.

efficiency, *n* – one-room flat.

eggnog, *n* – egg flip.

eggplant, *n* – aubergine.

eight-ball, *n* – the black ball in pool, which should remain on the table until the last. Hence **behind the eight-ball** means to be in a difficult situation.

electoral college, *n* – the body of electors who in theory elect the President, but in fact follow the dictates of the voting public.

elevated railroad or **elevated**, *n* – sometimes shortened to **el**. A railway running above and along a city street.

elevator, *n* – a lift.

Elks, *prop n* – a nation-wide fraternal order. Mostly small-city middle-class.

Emmy, *prop n* – the annual awards for excellence in television; television's equivalent of an Oscar.

Empire State, *prop n* – New York State; the sobriquet was bestowed by George Washington and has been flaunted since then.

end, *n* – a position in American football, the last man on the line. An **end run** is an attempt to carry the ball around the end, and is often used as a metaphor for an out-flanking manoeuvre of one kind or another.

endive, *n* – chicory.

engineer, *n* – this also means an engine-driver. Casey Jones, hailed in the song as 'the brave engineer', drove the engine.

english, *n* – a spin given to a ball when it is thrown or, in pool, hit with a cue.

English muffin, *n* – a flat roll for toasting, often eaten with butter and marmalade for breakfast. When my English wife visited an American drug-store for the first time with me, and I ordered breakfast, she was startled to hear the man behind the counter call out to the kitchen, 'Let's have two toasted English.'

enjoin, *v* – to forbid, usually by court order. The opposite of the British meaning.

enlisted man, *n* – anyone in the service who is not an officer. Sometimes abbreviated to **EM**.

eraser, *n* – rubber. A **rubber** is

a colloquial term for a condom. Ask at a stationer's for a rubber and you will be directed to a drugstore.

Erector set, *n* – a popular children's toy, similar to Meccano.

estate tax, *n* – death duties.

ethnics, *n* – Americans who identify with an ethnic subgroup, such as Polish-Americans and Italian-Americans.

European plan, *n* – a hotel rate for a room only, without food.

everglade, *n* – a tract of low, swampy land, characterized by clumps of tall grass and winding waterways, mostly in the South.

excise laws, *n* – the laws governing the sale of drink, when and how it may be sold as well as its manufacture, areas which in Britain are covered by the licensing laws.

explorer, *n* – a dental probe. The sharp instrument with which a dentist explores the mouth for cavities.

expressway, *n* – motorway.

F

fag or **faggot**, *n* (col) – homosexual. Probably the most common term for this. Alistair Cooke, in one of his 'Letter from America' broadcasts, recalls a conversation between an American and a British diplomat:

American: 'Do you know Lord —— by any chance?'

Englishman: 'Yes, known him all my life. He was my fag at Eton.'

American: 'Well! I'll say this for you British, you certainly are frank!'

fair-haired boy, *n* – blue-eyed boy, favourite.

fair trade, *n* – subject to resale price maintenance rules.

fairy, *n* – homosexual.

fall, *n* – autumn. Both words are used.

fall-guy, *n* – someone made to bear the consequence of something which was not his fault.

fanny, *n* – arse. The title of the British film *Fanny by Gaslight* was changed when it was shown in America.

fatback, *n* – the fatty meat from the upper side of pork.

fat cat, *n* (col) – a wealthy potential contributor to a cause.

faucet, *n* – tap.

favorite son, *n* – a candidate for national office proposed by a local delegation with local support.

fedora, *n* – a trilby hat. The name comes from the French play *Fédora* by Victorien Sardou. The famous actress Fanny Burnley played the heroine in New York, and wore a man's hat.

feisty, *adj* (col) – peppery, temperamental.

ferris wheel, *n* – the big wheel at a fairground.

field hockey, *n* – hockey. **hockey** means ice hockey.

fifth, *n* (col) – a bottle of spirits – it's a fifth of a gallon.

fig newton, *n* – a soft biscuit with a fig centre.

filling station, *n* – petrol station.

film chain, *n* – tele-cine, a device which projects and transmits television film.

fin, *n* (col) – a five-dollar bill.

finagel, *v* (col) – to get something by devious means. Pronounced 'finay-gel'.

fink, *n* – originally it was a labour term for a blackleg or strike-breaker, now a general term of abuse.

finnan haddie, *n* – smoked haddock. Actually, this is the old Scottish term.

firecracker, *n* – firework. Both words are used.

fireman, *n* – as well as a firefighter, this also means someone who tends a furnace, particularly on an old-fashioned steam locomotive. A **visiting fireman** is a visitor to town who must be taken around and shown the sights.

fire plug, *n* – a fire hydrant. Both terms are used.

first floor, *n* – ground floor. The first floor (British) is called the second floor, and so on.

first lady, *n* – the wife of the President of the United States.

fish story, *n* – a tall tale. Derives from the kind of story fishermen are supposed to tell.

five, *n* (col) – to **take five** means to take a five-minute break.

five and dime or **five and ten**, *n* – the chain stores such as Woolworth's that used to sell goods at five and ten cents. The term is still heard occasionally.

flack, *n* (col) – public relations man.

flapjack, *n* – griddle cake.

flashlight, *n* – torch. To an American, a torch has flames.

flatfoot, *n* (col) – a policeman. A genial word for him.

flier, *n* – a circular.

flip, *v* (col) – to be carried away with excitement, in any direction, i.e. it might be rapture or anger.

float, *n* – an ice cream drink.

floor lamp, *n* – standard lamp.

floor-walker, *n* – shop walker.

flophouse, *n* – doss house.

flub, *v* (col) – to botch up, make a mess of something.

flunk, *v* (col) – to fail an exam or course.

flutist, *n* – flautist.

fly or **pop fly**, *n* – in baseball, a ball hit high in the air, easy to catch.

fly boy, *n* – pilot.

Foggy Bottom, *prop n* – the old name of the section of land near the Potomac River on which the State Department is located, sometimes used as a synonym for the Department.

folks, *n* – people, or more specifically, relations, e.g. 'My wife's folks are coming over.'

food stamp, *n* – a stamp with which food can be purchased; these are issued as a form of welfare payments.

football, *n* – always American football, never soccer.

foot locker, *n* – a small locker in which belongings are kept in a barracks, so-called because it is kept at the foot of the bed.

footsie, *v* – to play footsie with a girl means to stroke her foot with one's own under the table or otherwise surreptitiously. Often used metaphorically, to mean making friendly overtures.

foreign service, *n* – the diplomatic service.

formula, *n* – a baby's liquid feed.

forty-niner, *n* – a gold prospector who went to California in the great 1849 gold rush.

four-alarm fire, *n* – a major fire in which the resources of four fire stations are called upon. Sometimes used metaphorically, about an event that raises a furore.

four flusher, *n* (col) – a faker, particularly someone who bluffs with a false claim. The term comes from poker, where it means someone pretending to hold a five-card flush when he really has only four of the cards.

four hundred, *n* – the social élite of a city. The term was coined in 1888 by one Ward McAllister, an arbiter of social distinctions, who said there were only 400 people in New York who really counted socially.

fox, *n* – an attractive girl. **foxy** is the adjective, meaning attractive, sexy.

frag, *v* (col) – to attack with murderous intent one's officer in the army. The term comes from the weapon most often used in such assaults in Vietnam, the fragmentation grenade.

frame house, *n* – a wooden house with a frame of weatherboard, more common in America than Britain.

frank, *n* (col) – frankfurter, or hot dog.

fraternity, *n* – a club at American universities, the members ('brothers') of which are bound together by rituals and symbols. These are less significant than they were, and have vanished from some campuses.

freebie, *n* – anything given away free.

free-load, *v* (col) – to eat and drink at someone else's expense. Also **free-loader,** *n*.

freeway, *n* – motorway.

freight car, *n* – goods wagon.

french fries, *n* – french fried potatoes, or chips, although they are usually thinner and crisper than British chips. **chips** in America are crisps.

french toast, *n* – bread dipped in egg and milk and sautéed, a breakfast food.

fresh, *adj* (col) – cheeky, impudent, as in 'Don't you get fresh with me, young man,' or, if the lady likes it, 'Ooh, aren't you fresh!'

freshman, *n* – a first-year student. This is also applied to some other fields; one speaks, for instance, of a freshman senator, meaning one serving his first term.

fresh paint, *n* – wet paint.

frog, *n* – crossing plate on a railway.

fruit, *n* – a male homosexual.

fruit bread, *n* – currant bread.

fruit cup, *n* – fruit cocktail.

full court press, *n* – all-out effort, a term from basketball.

funnies, *n* – the comic strips in a newspaper.

funny farm, *n* – a . psychiatric hospital.

G

gabfest, *n* (col) – a talking session. The phrase was first used in the early years of this century in an account of a long-winded session of Congress in the *St Louis Globe-Democrat*. As there are many German-Americans in the area, and the word is clearly coined from the German, it was taken up quickly.

gallon, *n* – 231 cubic inches; a British gallon is 277 cubic inches. Pints and quarts have different liquid and dry measures in America, but a gallon is only a liquid measure.

galluses, *n* – wide, brightly-coloured braces. 'Gallowses' is an old North country and Scottish word for braces; it comes from 'gallows', i.e. where one is strung up.

gam, *n* (col) – leg. One of those words that are used more by film publicists than in conversation.

gander, *n* – a look at something.

gangway!, *interj* – called out as an order, this means 'Clear a path, make way!' As in the line in Marc Connelly's play about a vision of heaven, *Green Pastures*, which Alexander Woollcott called the greatest entrance line in the American theatre, 'Gangway, folks! Gangway for the Lawd God Jehovah!'

garage sale, *n* – jumble sale.

garbage, *n* – rubbish. A **garbage can** is a dustbin.

garter snake, *n* – a common American snake, harmless, identifiable by three stripes around its body.

gas or **gasoline,** *n* – petrol.

gas or **gasser,** *n* (col) – something that produces happiness or merriment, like a party or a joke.

gassed, *adj* (col) – drunk.

gat, *n* (col) – gun. Mostly underworld slang.

gearshift, *n* – gear lever.

German shepherd, *n* – an Alsatian dog. This was also the term used in Britain until the First World War, when the identification of some of Man's best friends with the Hun caused offence; the name was changed and the old one is now hardly used outside Cruft's.

get off, *v* (col) – to have an orgasm.

Gibson girl, *n* – the idealized American girl of the 1890s, as created by the illustrator Charles Dana Gibson.

Gideon Bible, *n* – a Bible placed in every hotel room in America by the Gideon Society, a society of Christian commercial travellers.

gidget, *n* – a pert, attractive girl.

gimp, *n* (col) – a cripple. **gimpy** means lame.

gin, *n* – a machine for separating seed from cotton, the invention of which, in the early nineteenth century, created the South's cotton-exporting economy. The word is a corruption of 'engine'.

Girl Scout, *n* – Girl Guide.

gizmo, *n* (col) – a mechanical whatchamacallit.

glad hand, *n* – an effusive greeting.

glee club, *n* – a club for choral singing.

glitch, *n* (col) – a hitch, a bug. The word comes from the aerospace industry.

glop, *n* (col) – 1. any semiviscous liquid. 2. sentimental slush.

glory hole, *n* – a spare room where things are stored. The term comes from gold and silver mining, where it meant the mine shaft that contains the rich seam.

glove, *n* (col) – condom. 'No glove, no love,' a girl tells her partner in *The World According to Garp* by John Irwin.

glue factory, *n* – knackers' yard.

gobbledygook, *n* (col) – jargon, difficult to understand. Evidently the sound made by a turkey, the word was coined by a Texan with the very Texan-sounding name of Maury Maverick, when he was head of the Small War Plants Corporation, a government agency, in Washington during the Second World War. This was in an edict on bureaucratic jargon which contained the splendidly frontier-style statement 'Anyone using the words "activation" or "implementation" will be shot.'

gofer, *n* (col) – a dogsbody in an office who is sent to 'go for' coffee, messages, etc., for the others.

go-go, *adj* (col) – characterized by great energy and movement. A newspaper referred recently to 'an exciting, go-go baseball team', and a dynamic company's shares as 'go-go shares'.

goldbrick, *n* (col) – a loafer, one who shirks work.

gondola, *n* – a flat railway goods wagon with no sides or low sides.

goof, *v* (col) – to make a mistake.

goof ball, *n* (col) – 1. an eccentric. 2. a sleeping pill, or tranquilliser, or pill made from narcotics.

goof off, *v* (col) – avoid work, slack off.

gook, *n* (col) – an Asian, a racist term that first became common among US troops in the Korean War, though it pre-dates this.

goon, *n* – thug.

goose egg, *n* – 1. a zero. 2. a bump on the head; usually used about children.

GOP, *n* (abbr) – the Republican Party. The letters stand for Grand Old Party.

gopher, *n* – a rodent or ground squirrel found mostly on the prairie.

Gotham, *prop n* – New York City.

gotten, *v* – the past participle of

'to get', e.g. 'I'd gotten a prize for English.' It was British in Shakespeare's day.

grab bag, *n* – lucky dip.

grade, *n* – 1. a one-year stage in school. The American starts school at the age of six in the first grade, and leaves it twelve years later in the 12th grade. 2. a mark in school; a 'good grade' in an exam means a high mark. 3. gradient.

grade at, *adj* – at ground level. Used mostly in building.

grade crossing, *n* – level crossing.

grade school, *n* – primary school.

graft, *n* – corruption in public office.

graham cracker, *n* – a soft wholemeal biscuit.

grandfather clause, *n* – a clause in a law that creates an exemption because of previously existing circumstances. This sounds obscure, but an example may clarify it. When, in Britain recently, the Conservative Government abolished subsidies for direct grant schools, it said that those students who were already receiving subsidies for their school fees should continue to receive them. This provision would be called a grandfather clause.

grand jury, *n* – a jury at a preliminary hearing.

grandstand play, *n* – something done to impress an audience.

graveyard shift, *n* – night shift.

greaser, *n* (col) – an insulting term for a Mexican or other Latin.

greasewood, *n* – a low, stiff shrub found mostly in the West.

Green Mountain State, *prop n* – Vermont.

green thumbs, *n* – green fingers.

gridiron, *n* – a football field, often used in sports, reporting as a synonym for the game, e.g. 'It was a weekend of gridiron thrills . . .'

gridlock, *n* – a traffic jam that extends in all directions.

grifter, *n* (col) – a con man or card sharp.

grind, *n* (col) – a hard worker. Mostly a college term.

grip, *n* – suitcase.

grippe, *n* – influenza.

grits, *n* – coarsely-ground grains of maize, wheat or rice. A characteristically Southern food.

gross, *adj* – disgusting in some way. To **gross out** is to disgust, as in 'That grosses me out!'

groundhog, *n* – a woodchuck, a species of marmot. **groundhog day,** *n* – 2 or 14 February, depending on the part of the country. According to rural lore, this is the day that the groundhog ends its hibernation, and the day's weather is a sign of the season to come.

ground meat, *n* – minced meat. **ground round** is best minced meat.

ground rules, *n* – the rules for a particular occasion. This is actually a baseball term, meaning the special rules for a particular stadium or field.

ground wire, *n* – earth wire.

grubs, *n* – dirty old clothes, especially cut-off jeans.

grunt, *n* (col) – a Vietnam War word for a combat foot soldier, this shows signs of a continuing civilian career as a word for a dogsbody, someone who does the dirty work. William Safire, the syndicated columnist and word-watcher, has spotted the derivation **gruntwork**, meaning the dreary chores.

gubernatorial, *adj* – referring to a state governor or his activities.

guinea, *n* (col) – a racist term for an Italian or Italian-American.

Gulf states, *n* – nothing to do with the Persian Gulf, but the American states on the Gulf of Mexico.

Gulla, *n* – blacks living on a coastal strip in South Carolina and Georgia, and their dialect, which contains many West African words and hence is of interest to linguists. The word may be a corruption of 'Ngola', a tribe in what is now Angola.

gumbo, *n* – okra, a plant of West African origin with gummy pods used as food. Also a kind of stew containing okra, identified by the principal other ingredients, e.g. chicken gumbo, shrimp gumbo. From Louisiana and thereabouts. The word is pure Bantu.

gumshoe, *n* (col) – someone who moves about quietly and secretively, especially a detective.

gung ho, *adj* (col) – aggressively energetic, very keen. It is a Chinese phrase that during the Second World War was the motto of an American marine commando-style unit.

gussy up, *v* – to prettify, tart up.

gut, *adj* – visceral, moved by primitive emotions, as in 'gut reaction' and 'gut fight'. **gut course**, *n* – an easy course at university.

gyp, *n* and *v* – cheat, swindle. Used light-heartedly, or for small matters. 'Neil, you gypped me out of a point. You have 16 and I have 11.' – from *Goodbye, Columbus* by Philip Roth.

H

haberdasher, *n* – men's outfitter.

hack, *n* – 1. – a horse-drawn vehicle, e.g.:
Bring out your rubber-tyred hearses,
Bring out your four-wheeled hacks.
'Cos I'm taking my man to the graveyard
And I ain't gonna bring him back.
– from the song 'Frankie and Johnny'.
2. (col) taxi.

hack it, *v* (col) – to cope, to deal with a situation, usually a difficult one.

hairy, *adj* (col) – dangerous, close to the edge.

half-and-half, *n* – 1. in a supermarket, a mixture of milk and cream, used in coffee. 2. in a brothel, fellatio plus intercourse.

hamburger meat, *n* – minced meat.

hand, *n* – a worker, particularly on a farm or ranch.

handball, *n* – a game played by hitting a ball against a wall. An urban pastime.

hands-on, *adj* – practical involvement as training. **hands-on learning** about a machine means learning that includes experience of operating it.

hang in there, *v* (col) – to stay the course, stick it out.

hang loose, *v* – adopt a free, relaxed style. A term of the 1960s.

happening, *adj* (col) – jumping, lively, e.g. 'It was a happening evening.' A word that, among the young, has moved eastwards from California. In some circles, 'Where's the haps?' is the equivalent of 'Where's it at?'

happy hunting ground, *n* – heaven as envisaged by some Western Indian tribes. 'He went to the happy hunting ground' is a cute way of saying he died.

hard-hat, *n* – construction worker, used as socio-political shorthand for manual workers with reactionary views.

hard-nosed, *adj* (col) – tough-minded, hard-headed. There is no precise British synonym, but, oddly, an approximate antonym in 'toffee-nosed'.

hard-on, *n* (col) – an erection. 'Doctor, just saying her name, just bringing her to mind, gives me a hard-on on the spot!' – from *Portnoy's Complaint* by Philip Roth.

hard sauce, *n* – a sauce for desserts made with butter and sugar and, usually, cream and flavouring.

hard-shell Baptist, *n* – a fundamentalist Baptist, clinging dogmatically to traditional beliefs.

hash, *n* – 1. minced meat mixed with potatoes, browned. 2. a mess.

hash house, *n* – a cheap restaurant. A **hash slinger** is a waiter or waitress in one.

hash over, *v* (col) – to talk over something.

hassle, *n* – quarrel, row.

hay-maker, *n* (col) – knock-out punch.

hayride, *n* – a ride taken by a picnic party in a large wagon filled with hay. A traditional social event in rural America, and despite verbal associations, usually a decorous one.

hayseed, *n* – country bumpkin.

haze, *v* – to subject a newcomer to tricks or teasing.

head, *n* – 1. the toilet, a US navy term (it is also a Royal Navy term), but now used more widely. 2. to **give head** to someone means to practise fellatio or cunnilingus.

heater, *n* – gas or electric fire. A fire in America has flames.

heavy, *adj* (col) – serious, important.

heist, *v* (col) – to steal.

hell's kitchen, *n* – any district with a reputation for crime and violence.

help, *n* – a servant or servants, e.g. 'The help will take care of it.'

hemlock, *n* – a kind of fir or spruce tree, far from poisonous. American schoolchildren may not always know about the death of Socrates, but many learn the opening words of Longfellow's *Evangeline*: 'This is the forest primeval, The murmuring pines and the hemlock . . .'

hen party, *n* – a girls-only party.

hero sandwich, *n* – a section of French loaf plus a lot of filling, making a huge sandwich.

hex, *n* and *v* – malevolent magic spell; or to cast such a spell.

hick, *n* and *adj* – rural or small-town, and unsophisticated, or such a person.

hickey, *n* (col) – the mark left by a love bite.

hickory, *n* – a native American tree of the walnut family, with strong wood. Andrew Jackson was known as 'Old Hickory', because of his stubbornness and strength; traditionally, a schoolteacher's cane, when such things were allowed, was a **hickory stick.**

high, *adj* and *n* – a state of exhilaration, as, though not necessarily, caused by drink or drugs.

highball, *n* – any whisky and soda or ginger ale.

highboy, *n* – tallboy.

high-hat, *v* (col) – to snub or treat condescendingly.

high-muck-a-muck, *n* (col) – a person of assumed or real importance. The phrase takes him down a peg. It comes from the Chinook Indian.

high on the hog, *adj* (col) – off the fat of the land.

high roller, *n* (col) – a big-spending gambler. The word **roller** refers to rolling the dice in a game of craps. See CRAPS.

high school, *n* – secondary school covering roughly the ages fourteen to eighteen.

high-tail, *v* (col) – to rush, go somewhere rapidly.

high-toned, *adj* – socially refined or perhaps snobbish.

high yellow, *adj* (col) – of a black girl, light-skinned and sexually attractive.

hike, *n* – a boost, a rise; e.g. 'Auto Workers Seek 9 p.c. Pay Hike' – *New York Times* headline.

hike, *v* – a motion in American football in which the centre flips the ball back between his legs to one of the backs, starting the play.

hipped, *past part* – fanatically keen, as in 'He was hipped on astral consciousness.'

hit, *v* (col) – to turn to or take up; to **hit the road** means to go away or travel, to **hit the bottle** means to take to drink, to **hit the sack** means to go to bed. By itself, 'Hit it!' is an encouraging exhortation meaning something like 'Go man go!'

hit, *n* (col) – a murder; an underworld term.

hitch, *v* (col) – marry. Used without an object, e.g. 'We got hitched,' never 'He hitched her.'

hoagy, *n* – a hero sandwich. See HERO SANDWICH.

hockey, *n* – this means ice hockey. The other kind is called **field hockey.**

hog tied, *adj* – figuratively, tied up and helpless.

ho-hum, *adj* – banal, monotonous.

home free, *adj* – home and dry.

homely, *adj* – plain featured, or downright ugly. This meaning has now overcome any others. More than one Englishman being entertained in an American home has startled fellow guests by describing his hostess as 'a very homely lady'.

homemaker, *n* – housewife. This word was introduced into the language by women's magazines over the past twenty-five years, in the belief that the word 'housewife' implied a menial or subservient status. The change was not a precursor of women's lib, since it would change the status rather than the role.

home run, *n* – A hit in baseball that takes the batter right around the bases to score a run. Often reduced to **homer.**

homesteader, *n* – one of the settlers in the old West who took advantage of the Homestead Act, which gave away land in order to encourage settlement of the West.

hominy grits, *n* – boiled, coarsely-ground maize. A Southern and usually rural dish.

honcho, *n* (col) – a boss, usually of one particular section rather than a supremo. This seems to be an adaptation of a Japanese word brought back by GIs.

honky, *n* (col) – a common black American term for a white man.

Honorable, *adj* – an honorific before the name of a senior office-holder, e.g. a congressman or state governor. It is never used for the President or a cabinet member.

honors system, *n* – the system at university by which students taking an exam are freed from supervision and can come and go as they please, and sign a pledge that they have not cheated.

hooch, *n* (col) – spirits.

hood, *n* – 1. a car's bonnet. 2.

(col) a gangster, abbreviation of 'hoodlum'.

hoof and mouth disease, *n* – foot and mouth disease.

hooky, *n* (col) – truant. To play truant is to **play hookey**.

hoosegow, *n* – jail. A Western word, from the Spanish *juzgado*, meaning 'judged'.

Hoosier, *adj* – native to Indiana.

hootchy-kootchy, *n* – an erotic dance, modest by today's standards but daring in earlier years when the dance was in vogue.

hooters, *n* (col) – breasts.

hop, *n* – a dance, as an event to go to. A **sock hop** is an informal dance.

hope chest, *n* – bottom drawer.

Horatio Alger, *prop n* – the author of many boys' books around the turn of the century in which the hero as a boy was honest, upright and hard-working and rose to wealth and success, hence, the archetype of such a rags-to-riches story. 'It has its Horatio Alger heroes and its robber barons, but no empire builders.' – from *Desert Challenge* by Robert Lilliard.

horn, *n* – 1. telephone. 2. the pommel of a saddle.

hornswoggle, *v* (col) – to bamboozle, a rural-sounding word.

horny, *adj* (col) – randy.

horse play, *n* – friendly, male rough play. **horsing around,** *v* – indulging in horse play.

hoser, *n* – someone who acts clownishly. A young people's word.

hostler, *n* – ostler.

hot foot, *n* – a savage practical joke which consists in attaching a match to a person's shoe when he is not looking and lighting it.

hots, *n* (col) – sexual excitement or desire, e.g. 'Unfortunately, he's got the hots for his boss's secretary,' as I heard someone say.

house mother, *n* – warden in a women's hall of residence.

housing project, *n* – a housing development or estate.

Hoyle, *prop n* – referring to Edmond Hoyle, an eighteenth-century Englishman more honoured abroad than at home, who compiled a book of standard rules for games: **according to Hoyle** means strictly according to the rules.

huckleberry, *n* – a small wild fruit, similar to a blueberry.

huckster, *n* – a hard-sell salesman. A fairground barker. Also used, ironically, for advertising executives.

huddle, *n* – in football, a brief conference of the team on the field to receive instructions on the next move. Hence, any secret planning conference.

humidor, *n* – cigar box.

hump, *v* (col) – to screw, have sexual intercourse with. Fairly rude.

hundredweight, *n* – . 100 pounds, not 112.

hunger, *n* (col) – something that is **from hunger** is awful.

hung jury, *n* – a jury that is divided and cannot reach a verdict.

hunk, *n* (col) – a gorgeous, attractive man.

hunker down, *v* – originally an old Scottish term, it means to squat on one's haunches.

Recently it has come to mean also to sit around and talk something out.

hunkered, *adj* – squatting on one's haunches.

hunkie, *n* (col) – an immigrant from Hungary.

hunky-dory, *adj* (col) – fine, very satisfactory.

hunting, *n* – hunting with a gun, shooting.

hurdy gurdy, *n* – barrel organ.

hush puppy, *n* – a small, deep fried cornmeal cake. Southern.

hustler, *n* – if a man, one who lives on his wits, or alternatively a male prostitute. If a woman, usually a prostitute.

hype, *v* and *n* (col) – to inject with extra vitality or strength. Clearly a word from drug users' jargon. As a noun, it means something artificial, created for effect, such as a strong line of sales talk.

I

iceberg lettuce, *n* – similar to a Webb's lettuce, but very crisp.

icebox, *n* – still used for a refrigerator.

iffy, *adj* – hypothetical.

incorporated, *adj* – limited, as in a limited company. **Inc.** after the firm's name is the equivalent of Ltd.

Indian giver, *n* (col) – someone who gives something and then asks for it back. A juvenile term.

information, *n* – directory inquiries, on the telephone.

installment plan, *n* – hire purchase.

instructor, *n* – a junior university teacher.

intern, *n* – houseman in a hospital.

intramural, *adj* – within one school or university, as 'intramural sports'.

Ivy League, *prop n* and *adj* – eight major universities in the Northeastern states with high academic and social status. Originally they were members of an athletic league with that name. The term often refers to a style of well-bred confidence that is supposedly associated with these institutions.

J

jack, *n* (col) – money. A truncated version of an old maxim comes out as 'All work and no play makes jack.' – from *Comfort Me With Apples* by Peter de Vries.

jackass, *n* – a male donkey. Colloquially, an idiot.

jackhammer, *n* – pneumatic drill.

jacklight, *n* – a portable lantern such as is used in camping.

jack off, *v* (col) – masturbate. A variation of jerk off.

jack rabbit, *n* – a large hare found in Western states.

jag, *n* – a prolonged and unstoppable bout of drinking, or of some kind of emotional behaviour. 'Florence got regular crying jags, and the men sought to cheer or comfort her.' – from *Big Blonde* by Dorothy Parker.

jam, *n* – thick jam with pieces of fruit in it, similar to preserves. British-style jam is called jelly.

janitor, *n* – caretaker.

jap, *n* – an acronym of Jewish-American princess, it in fact means any spoiled girl, Jew or Gentile, raised in the belief that she is entitled to the best of everything. A joke that gives the flavour of the creature:
What does a jap make for dinner? – Reservations.

java, *n* (col) – coffee.

jawbone, *v* – to talk tough with a view to persuading. 'There is every possibility, particularly with the militant miners, that long and bitter strikes will be the response to Government jawboning.' – report from London in the *New York Times*.

jazzed, *adj* (col) – keen, ready to go.

jello, *n* – jelly. A brand name that has become a generic word.

jelly, *n* – jam.

jelly roll, *n* – 1. swiss roll. 2. sexual intercourse, and particularly, the rotating of the pelvis during intercourse. It is presumably from this, rather than a kind of dessert, that the great jazz pianist Jelly Roll Morton took his name.

jerk, *n* – stupid person. A **soda jerk**, which has no pejorative connotation, means a man who serves behind the counter at a soda fountain. The phrase comes from the jerking motion with which he draws the drinks.

jerk off, *v* (col) – masturbate.

jerkwater, *adj* – small and insignificant, used mostly about a place.

jigaboo, *n* (col) – a black, a

racist term. Sometimes shortened to **jig**.

jigger, *n* – a tot, as of spirits.

jimmy, *n* – jemmy.

jitney, *n* – local transport for short journeys.

job action, *n* – industrial action at plant level.

jock, *n* (col) – a keen athlete. Derived from jockstrap. Mostly a campus and service term.

john, *n* (col) – toilet.

John Doe, *n* – 1. an average American. 2. a person of unknown identity in legal proceedings. In this case, the unknown person is entered in court records as 'John Doe'.

John Hancock, *n* (col) – signature. Derives from the fact that John Hancock's signature features prominently on the Declaration of Independence.

joiner, *n* – someone with a propensity for joining clubs and other organizations.

josh, *v* (col) – to tease, subject to light banter.

jug, *n* and *v* (col) – jail.

jugs, *n* (col) – breasts.

jumper, *n* – pinafore.

jumping rope, *n* – skipping rope.

jump suit, *n* – playsuit.

June bug, *n* – any of various large beetles of the genus *Phyllophaga*.

jungle bunny, *n* (col) – a black. An insult. The term has been given wide currency by the character in the TV comedy series *All in the Family* modelled on Britain's Alf Garnett.

junior, *n* – a student in the third year of his or her four-year course at secondary school or university.

junior college, *n* – an educational institution that offers studies equivalent to the first two years at university, and also, often, adult education.

junk food, *n* – food with no nutritional content.

justice of the peace, *n* – an official similar to a JP in Britain except that he can also perform marriages. Hence, in romantic story and song, to go and look for a justice of the peace means to set out to get married.

K

kaffeeklatsch, *n* – a social gathering for coffee and a chat, typically among housewives.

kazoo, *n* – a crude, home-made musical instrument consisting of a tube with a taut wire. A child's toy.

keister, *n* (col) – backside. This word had slipped out of use, but was revived by President Reagan when he said on television that he was 'fed up to the keister' with anti-nuclear demonstrators.

kerosene, *n* – paraffin.

kettle, *n* – a metal vessel for boiling liquid. The particular kind that is a kettle in Britain is called a **tea kettle.**

Kewpie doll, *n* – a small celluloid doll, a trade name that has become a generic term. Sometimes applied to a cute-looking, plastic-y female.

key punch, *n* – card punch.

kibbitz, *v* (col) – to give advice, requested or not, as to a player in a card game. Like many American colloquialisms, this comes from Yiddish. Not to be confused with a collective settlement in Israel.

kickback, *n* (col) – money exchanged in a business deal that is paid illicitly. If a buyer for a firm places an order with a company in return for a bribe

of 2 per cent of the price of the order, that 2 per cent is the kickback.

kicky, *adj* – exciting, providing a kick.

kike, *n* (col) – Jew, an insulting, racist term.

kitchen cabinet, *n* – a close group of presidential advisers chosen on a personal basis.

kitty corner, *n* – see CATER-CORNER.

klutz, *n* (col) – an awkward, clumsy person. **klutzy** is the adjective.

knee pants, *n* – short trousers. As 'My mama done tol' me/ When I was in knee pants . . .' – from the song 'Blues in the Night'.

knickers, *n* – baggy trousers tucked in below the knee. They were standard boys' wear in America for many years and are still seen. Named after the Knickerbockers, the original Dutch settlers of New York, then New Amsterdam, whose traditional garb they were.

knock up, *v* (col) – to get with child. A British girl visiting America told friends throughout one day that she was tired because the hotel porter had knocked her up early in the morning. The responses varied from 'Gee, that's awful!' to 'But how can you tell so *soon*?'

know-nothings, *n* – historically, the Native American Party in the mid-nineteenth century, a bigoted group dedicated to preserving American virtues against immigration. It was conspiratorial in style, and took its nickname from the insistence of officers when questioned that they knew nothing. The term is sometimes used in political abuse today.

kook, *n* – an eccentric or zany person; not necessarily pejorative. Rhymes with 'fluke', and probably derives from 'cuckoo'.

kooky, *adj* – eccentric, nutty.

KP or **kitchen police,** *n* – an assignment to clean in the kitchen. A service term.

kvetch, *v* and *n* – to complain. From the Yiddish. As a noun, it means someone who is always complaining.

L

Labor Day, *prop n* – the first Monday in September, always a national holiday. For most Americans, the three-day Labor Day weekend marks the end of summer.

labor union, *n* – trade union (for a note on the significance of the difference in terminology, see 'trade union' in the British/Americansection).

ladybug, *n* – ladybird.

lame duck, *n* and *adj* – in politics, a person whose term of office is due to end soon, and has therefore lost much of his authority. A lame duck President is one whose successor has already been elected.

landing gear, *n* – an aeroplane's undercarriage.

land patent, *n* – title deed to a plot of land.

lay, *v* – to have sexual intercourse with. This word has now been absorbed into British speech, yet not altogether. In American, the verb can be used in either direction, i.e. he lays her or she lays him; a man may speak of **getting laid.** The classic double entendre employing this word is still Dorothy Parker's 'If all the girls who ever danced in the Ziegfeld Follies were laid end to end, I wouldn't be surprised.'

leatherneck, *n* – a US Marine. Seen mostly in newspapers.

left field, *n* – out in left field, originally a baseball term, means beyond what is reasonable, too far out to be considered seriously.

letter, *n* – in campus terminology, the initial of the university on a sweater, denoting that the person is a member of a sports team. Getting it is an achievement.

levee, *n* – an embankment on a river built to prevent flooding. As the song goes: 'Waitin' on the levee, waitin' for the Robert E. Lee.'

leverage, *n* – gearing. The ratio between a company's capital and money borrowed. A financial term.

L hook, *n* – a square dress hook.

license plate, *n* – like a number plate on a car, except that it must be changed when the licence is renewed.

life preserver, *n* – a life jacket or life belt.

lightning bug, *n* – glow worm.

lily, *n* (col) – a sissy, a weak or effeminate man.

lima bean, *n* – a common vegetable, like a broad bean only softer.

limburger cheese, *n* – a cheese

known for its smell, a byword for strong odour.

limit line, *n* – the solid white line on a road delimiting a pedestrian crossing.

limp-wrist, *n* and *adj* (col) – male homosexual.

liverwurst, *n* – liver sausage.

loaded, *adj* (col) – 1. rich. 2. drunk.

loafer, *n* – a loose shoe without laces, a casual.

loan, *v* – either to lend or to borrow.

local, *n* – a trade union branch.

locate, *v* – to settle in a home or job. 'Are you located yet?' to a new arrival means 'Have you got a place to live?' or 'Have you found a job?'

loco, *adj* (col) – crazy.

locomotive, *n* – a mass cheer performed in unison that spells out a word, starting slowly and increasing in tempo like a loco-motive engine starting up.

locoweed, *n* – a weed found in the Southwest that gives animals brain disease when they eat it.

loft, *v* – to hoist or put aloft. 'Railguns could loft objects into orbit,' *New York Times* headline, 22 November 1980.

loge, *n* – the front of the dress circle at the theatre.

log-roll, *v* – to do a favour in return for a favour. Used often in politics. It comes from the pioneering days. A man could chop down trees and saw them up into logs to build his cabin, but could not roll them to the site himself. He would seek his neighbour's help on the basis of 'You help roll my logs and I'll help roll yours.'

Lone Star State, *prop n* – Texas. The phrase comes from the state flag, and the single star marks the fact that Texas was an independent republic for ten years, from 1836.

longshoreman, *n* – a docker who loads and unloads ships.

lot, *n* – a plot of land. Often used in combination, e.g. **sandlot, parking lot.**

lounge jacket, *n* – smoking jacket.

lounge suit, *n* – Quite different from the British, it is a woman's pyjama-type suit, literally for lounging in.

lowboy, *n* – a low dressing table with drawers.

lox, *n* – smoked salmon.

luau, *n* – a Hawaiian barbecue, a form of social entertaining.

luck out, *v* (col) – to get by through luck, to have a lucky stroke.

lulu or **looloo,** *n* (col) – something extraordinary in some way or another. 'That's a lulu!' means the same as 'That's really something!'

lumber, *n* – timber. A **lumber-jack** is a man who chops down trees.

lumberjacket, *n* – a heavy woollen jacket.

lumps, *n* (col) – metaphorically, bruises. If someone loses badly in a game or other situation, it may be said that he 'got his lumps'.

lunch pail, *n* – the container in which a man takes his lunch to work.

lunkhead, *n* (col) – a thick-headed person.

lush, *n* (col) – a drunkard.

lye, *n* – caustic soda or similar.

M

Ma Bell, *prop n* (col) – the telephone system or the telephone company, A.T.&T., which used to be called the Bell Telephone Company.

mace, *n* – a riot gas used by many American police forces, similar to CS gas. It is a trade name but has become a generic word, and even a verb, to mace.

mackinaw, *n* – a short, heavy woollen coat usually with a plaid design, typically worn for rough outdoor wear. The word used to mean a heavy woollen blanket given by the US Government to the Indians, which was named after an island at the junction of Lakes Erie and Huron where these were distributed.

mad, *adj* (col) – angry. It is usually used in a light vein rather than about very serious or weighty matters. Grammatically, it is used as an exact equivalent of 'angry', e.g. 'He'll get mad if he hears about it,' never 'He'll go mad.' This is contained in the first known glossary of American words, published as a series of articles in 1781 by John Witherspoon, a Scottish academic who was a member of the Continental Congress.

Madison Avenue, *prop n* – the advertising world. This is actually a New York street that contains many advertising agencies.

mad money, *n* – money that a girl may keep in reserve when she goes out with a man in case she **gets mad** at him and has to make her own way home.

maid of honor, *n* – bridesmaid; the bride's principal attendant at the wedding ceremony, customarily an unmarried sister or friend.

mail, *n* – post, also **mailman, mailbox** (the latter has two meanings: where one posts letters, and the box outside a home where letters are delivered). But the service is the post office, and so is the place.

Main Street, *prop n* – the high street; the term often stands for small-town America.

maître d., *n* – a common term for *maître d'hôtel,* or head waiter. Pronounced 'mayter dee'.

major, *n* – at university, one's subject of principal study; sometimes used about a student, e.g. 'She was a crazy mathematics major from the Wharton School of Business who could not count to 28 each month without getting into trouble.' – from *Catch-22* by Joseph Heller.

make, *v* – 1. to get into, as 'He made the football team,' or 'He made the sports page.' 2. seduce.

makefast, *n* – any structure to which a ship or boat is tied up.

make out, *v* (col) – to succeed sexually; also, to snog or pet (see PET).

Malemute, *prop n* – an Eskimo tribe. Also a breed of dog, originally from Alaska.

malted milk or **malted,** *n* – a sweet, rich drink made of milk, ice cream, flavouring, and malt powder made of evaporated milk and malted cereals.

Manhattan, *prop n* – 1. the island that is the central part of New York city. 2. a popular American cocktail made of rye whisky, sweet vermouth and bitters, served with a cherry.

manifest destiny, *n* – the doctrine promulgated first in the 1840s that it was the 'manifest destiny' – the phrase was used by a statesman of the period, John O'Sullivan – of the American people to govern the American continent; it was later extended by some to cover the destiny of the Anglo-Saxons to dominate the world.

Mann Act, *prop n* – the act of Congress that declares it a federal offence to take a woman across a state line for what in those days was termed 'immoral purposes'.

maple sugar, maple syrup, *n* – sugar and syrup made in New England from the sap of maple trees, with a distinctive and delicious flavour.

marguerita, *n* – a popular cocktail with a base of tequila, the Mexican spirit.

market, *v* – to shop. An American housewife will say, 'I'm going to do some marketing.'

martini, *n* – the most popular American cocktail, often called a 'dry martini' made of three (or more) parts gin to one part dry vermouth, usually served with an olive. Among other fulsome tributes: 'The proper union of gin and vermouth is a great and sudden glory; it is one of the happiest marriages on earth.' – Bernard de Voto.

Mary Jane, *prop n* (col) – marijuana. A play on the word.

mash note, *n* – a love letter, a somewhat dated term.

mason, *n* – anyone who works with stone or bricks.

Mason-Dixon line, *n* – the traditional dividing line between the Northern and Southern states, actually the southern boundary of Pennsylvania. Used frequently in a geographical, political or social context. It is named after two English surveyors who drew the line in the 1760s, Charles Mason and Jeremiah Dixon.

Masonite, *prop n* – fibreboard. This is a brand name that has become a part of the language.

match, *v* – to match coins or bills in a kind of heads-or-tails game.

math, *n* – maths.

matron of honor, *n* – similar to **maid of honor,** only she is married.

maverick, *n* – a cow that has wandered away from the herd.

Hence by extension, anyone who leaves a group (such as a political party) to take a solitary stance.

max, *n* – **to the max** means to the limit. Mostly young people's use.

mayor, *n* – a municipal official elected directly, and with far more powers than a mayor in Britain.

mazuma, *n* (col) – money.

MD, *n* (abbr) – medical doctor, a common term for a qualified physician.

mean, *adj* – nasty. It does not mean specifically stingy.

measure, *n* – a bar in music.

meat ax, *n* – any crude instrument wielded with a heavy hand, e.g. an American reporter complaining: 'He edited my story with a meat ax.'

Medal of Honor, *prop n* – the highest award for bravery. Also called the **Congressional Medal of Honor.**

medicine ball, *n* – a weighted ball about the size of a football, used in exercises.

Memorial Day, *prop n* – the day on which America's war dead are commemorated, 30 May, a public holiday in most states.

mesa, *n* – a high, narrow plateau with steep sides, a feature of the landscape in much of the Southwest. It is a Spanish word meaning 'table'.

mess kit, *n* – a set of eating utensils for travelling, used by the military and Boy Scouts.

meth, *n* – short for methamphetamine, or 'speed'. Not heard widely outside the company of users, but it is important to distinguish it from meths.

Mexican standoff, *n* – an impasse in which two enemies confront one another but neither can make a winning move.

mezzanine, *n* – dress circle in a theatre or cinema.

mickey finn, *n* (col) – a drink to which knock-out drops have been added.

Mickey Mouse, *adj* – trivial, lightweight. I heard someone say of a news organization: 'They use amateurs and pay them next to nothing; it's a Mickey Mouse outfit.'

milk run, *n* – in airmen's slang, a successful, uneventful flight.

Milquetoast, *prop n* – Casper Milquetoast is a comic-strip character who is the epitome of the mild-mannered weakling.

minor, *n* – in university, one's secondary subject, the opposite of major, e.g. 'His major was English literature, his minor political science.'

mint julep, *n* – a long, cool drink made with bourbon and mint, traditionally the drink of Southern planters.

Missouri, *prop n* (col) – a man from Missouri is, according to tradition, a sceptic who has to be shown something before he believes it. Hence, 'I'm from Missouri,' means 'I'll believe it when I see it.'

Mister Charlie, *n* (col) – a black term for a white man.

mitt, *n* – 1. a baseball glove, a huge padded glove made for catching rather than throwing. 2. (col) a hand.

mixer, *n* – 1. a sociable or gregarious person. 'He's a very sensitive boy. He's never been a terribly good mixer with other boys.' – from *The Catcher in the Rye* by J.D. Salinger. 2. a college dance, intended to bring people together. 3. something added to spirits, such as soda or ginger ale.

mixologist, *n* – a bartender, a circumlocutory term sometimes used for comic effect. (An American bartender, unlike most in England, spends much of his time mixing cocktails.)

mob, *n* – usually, a criminal gang. **mobster** means a member of a gang.

mobile home, *n* – a house on wheels, often much larger than a caravan. It is built so that it can be moved from one site to another, but not to be in continuous motion.

mocking bird, *n* – a native American bird of the thrush family, that mimics other birds' sounds.

model T, *n* – a machine or system that works reliably but lacks luxury appurtenances or sophistication. The term comes from the model T Ford, the first-ever family car ('You can have it any colour providing it's black.' – Henry Ford), which occupies a special place in the American folk memory.

molasses, *n* – dark treacle.

Mollybolt, *prop n* – a holder for a screw in a wall, similar to a Rawlplug. As with the latter, this is a brand name that has become common usage.

mom, *n* – mum.

momentarily, *adv* – very soon, *in* a moment, not *for* a moment. (See MOMENTARILY in British/American section.)

Monday morning quarterback, *n* – a **quarterback** is the player on a football team who decides on tactics, so a Monday morning quarterback is someone who says at the office on Monday how the weekend's game should have been played. Hence, anyone who is wise after the event.

monkey, *n* – used in combination, someone who works at something with his hands; a **grease monkey** is a mechanic, a **powder monkey** in the navy is an explosives handler.

monkey wrench, *n* – an adjustable spanner.

mononucleosis, *n* – glandular fever.

moolah, *n* (col) – money.

mopboard, *n* – skirting board. Also called **baseboard**.

mortician, *n* – undertaker.

mosey, *v* – to stroll, go casually.

mossback, *n* and *adj* – a person of antiquated conservative views.

mother, *n* – 1. an abbreviation of mother-fucker, a term so obscene as to be beyond the bounds of native British speech. However, like most words of abuse, it can be used among males as a term of affection, particularly among blacks. 2. anything big or imposing. Stephen Fay, reviewing the first edition of this dictionary in the *Sunday Times*, recalled a dinner hostess in New York greeting him with, 'I hope you're hungry. I've got a mother of a steak for you.'

motorman, *n* – the driver of a tube train or tram.

mountain oyster, *n* – the cooked testicles of a sheep or bull, reckoned a delicacy in some rural areas.

mountain time, *n* – the time zone in the West Central United States.

mourners' bench, *n* – at revivalist religious meetings, a bench at the front set aside for mourners or penitent sinners.

movie, *n* – motion picture. A **movie theater** is a cinema.

moxie, *n* (col) – energy, spunk.

MP, *n* (abbr) – military policeman.

muff, *n* – female genitalia. Obscene.

muffler, *n* – silencer on a car.

mug-shot, *n* – a photograph of a person taken for official purposes.

mugwump, *n* – a political independent or a group standing between the two main parties. It was current about the turn of the century, as a description borne proudly. But then a critic defined it as a bird that sits on the fence, with its mug on one side and its wump on the other.

mule-skinner, *n* – mule-driver.

muley saw, *n* – a saw with a long stiff blade, with motion directed by clamps at each end, mounted on guide rails.

mulligan stew, *n* – Irish stew.

mums, *n* – chrysanthemums. Like 'chrysanths', this is an abbreviation.

mu-mu, *n* – a long, loose-fitting, Hawaiian-style dress.

murphy bed, *n* – a bed that folds back into a cupboard. Originally a trade name.

muskeg, *n* – a bog formed in a depression of land.

muskrat, *n* – a native North American rodent, an aquatic mammal with webbed feet and smooth, dark brown fur. **musquash** fur comes from one kind of muskrat.

muss, *v* – to mess up, make untidy. The air force general in *Dr. Strangelove*, talking about the prospects of a nuclear exchange with Russia, says: 'I don't say we wouldn't get our hair mussed, but we could get away with maybe 20 million dead.'

mutt, *n* (col) – a mongrel dog.

mutual fund, *n* – a unit trust fund.

N

narc or **nark,** *n* (col) – an agent of the Federal Narcotics Bureau.

natch, *adv* (col) – naturally, of course.

national guard, *n* – the military force of a state, composed of part-time soldiers, which becomes part of the national armed forces in time of war.

narly, *adj* (col) – fine, splendid. Mostly a teenage term.

Native American, *n* – American Indian.

navy yard, *n* – navy dockyard.

neat, *adj* – excellent. A young people's word.

nebbish, *n* (col) – a feeble, ineffectual person. From the Yiddish.

neckerchief, *n* – a small scarf worn at the throat.

nerd, *n* – a fool, and an unpleasant one at that.

nervy, *adj* – with a lot of nerve, impudent. A recent headline in *People* magazine talked about 'The Nervy Guy Who Preaches "Creative Intimidation" '; the adjective would hardly be appropriate to his theme if it had the British meaning.

newsboy, *n* – a boy who sells or delivers newspapers.

newsman, *n* – journalist.

nickel, *n* – a five-cent coin.

nickelodeon, *n* – 1. an early cinema, usually with an entrance price of a nickel. 2. a jukebox.

night crawler, *n* – a worm used as bait in fishing. One British motorist driving through an American small town, seeing this advertised on a sign, assumed it was a quaint term for a motel with places for late travellers.

nightgown, *n* – nightdress.

night letter, *n* – overnight telegram.

night school, *n* – evening classes.

night stick, *n* – a policeman's truncheon.

nip-and-tuck, *adj* – neck-and-neck.

nipple, *n* – it also means the teat of a baby's bottle. See NIPPLE in the British/American section.

Nisei, *n* – a first-generation Japanese-American.

nitty-gritty, *n* – the hard details, brass tacks.

no-go, *adj* – not in a condition to go ahead. The term comes from space launches.

no-no, *n* – something that should never be done under any circumstances.

normal school, *n* – teacher training college. They are rarely called this today, but many were a few years ago.

nosh, *n* – used in its correct Yiddish sense, unlike in Britain, to mean a light snack beteween meals.

notary public, *n* – commissioner for oaths.

notions, *n* – haberdashery and other small items.

nudnik, *n* (col) – a dreary person, a bore. Another Yiddish word. Leo Rosten, in *The Joys of Yiddish*, says the education explosion in America has thrown up a new word, **phudnik**, which means a nudnik with a PhD.

nuts, *n* (col) – testicles.

O

oatmeal, *n* – porridge.

obfuscate, *v* – to confuse or cloud an issue.

observation car, *n* – a railway carriage, usually at the end of the train, designed to give the passengers a good view of the scenery.

ofay, *n* – a common black term for a white. It is pig-Latin for foe, and this is popularly believed to be its derivation, but Dr Dalby (see under BUG) says it comes from Mandingo.

off, *v* (col) – kill. Underworld slang, probably black, which has emerged recently.

offshore fund, *n* – an investment fund based outside America, not subject to American financial laws, and not allowed to sell shares within the United States.

oilers, *n* – oilskins.

Okie, *n* – originally an Oklahoman who fled the dust bowl storms in the 1930s, it has come to mean any poor farmer.

Old Faithful, *prop n* – a geyser in the Yellowstone National Park that erupts every 57 minutes exactly. Hence, anything or anyone totally reliable.

old fashioned, *n* – a popular and colourful cocktail, consisting of bourbon, bitters, sugar and fruit. An **old fashioned glass** is not a piece of antique tableware, but a small glass with a flat heavy base, and about the volume of a wine glass, in which an old fashioned is properly served.

Old Glory, *prop n* – the American flag.

old money, *n* – wealth that has been in the family for generations. People with old money are the opposite of *nouveau riche*. 'The establishment is predominately Anglo-American, from long settled families with old money.' – from *The Diplomacy of Detente* by Coral Bell.

oleo, *n* – margarine. Short for oleo-margarine.

omnibus bill, *n* – a bill before Congress that links together several unconnected proposals.

one-horse town, *n* – a small and insignificant town. The first known use is in Mark Twain's *The Undertaker's Chat*: 'This poor little one-horse town.'

one-on-one, *adj* – person-to-person, although it is not used about a telephone call.

op-ed page, *n* – the page in a newspaper opposite the editorial page which carries signed columns and other articles of opinion.

open primary, *n* – a primary election (see PRIMARY) in which anyone can vote for any nominee regardless of party.

opine, *v* – to give an opinion.

orchestra, *n* – the front stalls in a theatre.

ordinance, *n* – by-law.

ornery, *adj* – cantankerous. Rural.

outfit, *n* – a group of people working together, or a unit in the army.

out-house, *n* – outdoor toilet.

outlet, *n* – electric power point.

outrider, *n* – a motor cyclist riding as escort.

out to lunch, *adj* – crazy, or simply unaware of what is going on around. The phrase implies that the brain has stopped working and taken a lunch-break.

overalls, *n* – a boiler suit.

overpass, *n* – a flyover.

oversight, *n* – this is often used as the past participle of 'oversee', producing some odd-looking sentences, e.g. 'A promising Congressional over-sight committee into CIA activities has emerged.' – J. Robert Schaetzel in the *International Herald Tribune*.

ox bow, *n* – a sharp bend in a river or the land enclosed in such a bend.

oyster cocktail, *n* – oysters served with trimmings.

P

Pacific time, *n* – the Westernmost of the four time zones in the continental United States, eight hours behind GMT.

pacifier, *n* – a baby's dummy.

pad, *n* (col) – the shared takings from bribes at a police station. The phrase **on the pad** came into general circulation with the Knapp Commission investigation into police corruption in New York City in 1971.

paddle, *v* – to spank with a paddle.

paddle tennis, *n* – a children's form of tennis played with paddles.

pallisade, *n* – a stretch of steep cliffs. To New Yorkers 'the Pallisades' is the long cliffs facing Manhattan along the Hudson River; to Californians it means the Pacific Pallisades near Los Angeles.

palooka, *n* (col) – a guy or fellow. Usually inferior. The term originally meant a broken-down boxer.

pancake turner, *n* – fish slice.

panhandle, *n* – a narrow projecting strip of territory, as the Texas panhandle and the Laos panhandle.

panhandler, *n* – a beggar.

pantiewaist, *n* – sissy. During the Second World War a pamphlet about Britain issued by the US Office of War Information for GIs stationed in the country put them right about their ally with the opening sentence: 'The English language was not spread from Alaska to Singapore by a nation of pantiewaists.'

pants, *n* – trousers. Pants in the English sense are **underpants** or **drawers**. See first page of Introduction.

pantyhose, *n* – tights. Tights refer to ballet tights.

paper, *n* – money.

paper-hanger, *n* – decorator.

paraffin, *n* – paraffin wax. What in Britain is paraffin is **kerosene** in America.

parakeet, *n* – budgerigar, and related small parrots.

parchisi, *n* – a dice and board game, originating in India, but popular in many American small towns.

parka, *n* – anorak. An Eskimo word.

parkerhouse roll, *n* – a kind of soft roll, created at the Parker House Hotel in Boston.

parking lot, *n* – car park.

parkway, *n* – a broad thoroughfare, usually landscaped with trees and plots of grass.

parlay, *n* – accumulator bet.

parlay, *v* (col) – to make money multiply.

parley, *n* – conference. This word is seen mostly in newsprint.

parlor car, *n* – a first-class railway carriage with individual armchair seats.

parochial school, *n* – church school, usually Roman Catholic.

party, *v* – to go to a lot of parties.

party-pooper, *n* (col) – someone who refuses to join in the fun.

pastie, *n* – a small covering for a woman's nipple, in some costumes.

pastrami, *n* – smoked beef, highly seasoned, popular as a sandwich filler.

patrolman, *n* – an ordinary policeman.

patrol wagon, *n* – black maria.

patsy, *n* (col) – someone who is being manipulated by others.

pay dirt, *n* – soil which contains valuable minerals, as found by a prospector. Much used metaphorically; e.g. 'Treasury investigators are striking pay dirt in their drive against tax evasion.' – *Chicago Daily News,* 1 August 1965.

payola, *n* (col) – money paid in bribes to obtain favours.

pay station, *n* – a telephone call box.

pea jacket, *n* – a navy-style duffel coat.

peasant, *n* (col) – an ignorant yokel, or someone acting in a boorish, ill-mannered way.

pecan, *n* – an American nut, similar to a walnut, popular as a flavouring.

pecker, *n* (col) – penis. The

Englishman in North America should beware of using the phrase 'Keep your pecker up.'

peeler, *n* – striptease dancer.

peg pants, *n* – tapered trousers.

pemmican, *n* – a concentrated mixture of dried lean meat and fat. An American Indian word, and originally, an American Indian food.

penny, *n* – cent.

persimmon, *n* – a native American fruit, orange-coloured and about the size of a plum.

pesky, *adj* (col) – irritating, troublesome.

pet, *v* – to snog plus. Although occasionally used by the ignorant as a synonym for 'neck', this word denotes slightly more advanced activity. As Frederic Morton explains in *The Art of Courtship,* 'Petting is necking with territorial concessions.'

Phi Beta Kappa, *prop n* – an academic fraternity restricted to those who graduate from university with the highest academic honours. A **Phi Beta Kappa key** is the key-shaped badge, customarily worn on a watch chain.

Philadelphia lawyer, *n* – a lawyer who is particularly wily. Oddly, the term seems to have originated in England. Mathews' *Dictionary of Americanisms* quotes a letter from London in an American Journal published in 1788 saying that people there were using the expression 'It would have puzzled a Philadelphia lawyer.' The correspondent wondered how the expression originated.

phonograph, *n* – record-player.

phooey!, *interj* – nuts! Childish.

phylactic, *n* – condom.

pianola, *n* – an automatic piano. Originally a trade name.

piazza, *n* – this also means a porch.

picayune, *adj* – trifling, petty. A picayune was a coin of low denomination in the Spanish settlements in North America.

pick, *n* – pickaxe.

pickerel, *n* – any of the smaller kinds of pike.

pick-up, *n* – it also means a pick-me-up.

pick-up truck, *n* – an open-back lorry.

picky, *adj* – choosy, difficult to please.

piece, *n* – gun.

piker, *n* – a mean, stingy person.

Pilgrim Fathers, *prop n* – the English Puritan colonists who founded the first colony in New England at Plymouth, Massachusetts, in 1620.

pinch hit, *v* – in baseball, to substitute for the batter; hence to substitute for someone in any job or role. Also **pinch hitter.**

pinkie, *n* – little finger.

pink slip, *n* – notice of dismissal.

pinochle, *n* – a popular card game.

pint, *n* – 28.87 cubic inches liquid measure or 33.6 cubic inches dry measure. There is only one British pint, 34.68 cubic inches; the British pint is used in Canada.

pipe story, *n* – a story said to be

true that is in fact fiction, like a pipe dream.

pissed, *adj* (col) – sometimes an abbreviation of 'pissed off', it never means drunk, as in British.

pit, *n* – 1. the part of an exchange devoted to special business, e.g. the **grain pit.** 2. the store of a fruit.

pit, *v* – to remove the stones from fruit such as cherries.

pitch, *n* – a line of sales talk.

pitcher, *n* – 1. jug. 2. in baseball, the man who throws the ball to the batter.

pitcher's mound, *n* – the slightly raised piece of ground on which the pitcher (see above) stands.

pitman, *n* – a connecting rod on a machine.

pizano, *n* (col) – friend. A newish, young people's word.

pizazz, *n* (col) – vigour, bounce. Occasionally spelt **pazazz.**

place, *n* – on the racecourse, coming in second, instead of second or third (see SHOW), as in Britain.

plank, *n* – a point in a political platform.

plate, *n* – the anode of a radio valve.

play, *n* – a team's action in American football; hence, a strategic move towards a goal.

plea bargaining, *n* – negotiation of an agreement between a defendant in court and the prosecution whereby the defendant pleads guilty to a reduced charge, saving the court some time and probably reducing his sentence.

plebe, *n* – first-year cadet at a military academy.

pledge, *v* – on campus, to commit oneself to join a fraternity or sorority, or to be so committed.

plotz, *v* (col) – collapse, fall down, fail catastrophically. **plotzed** can mean drunk.

plug, *n* – a piece of tobacco.

plug ugly, *n* – thug.

plurality, *n* – more votes than any other contender, but not an absolute majority. An American would say that the Conservatives, because they got fewer votes than Labour and the Alliance combined in 1983, won the election with a plurality.

pocket book, *n* – handbag.

pocket veto, *n* – a Presidential veto of a Congressional bill in which the President simply ignores it instead of, as in another form of veto, sending it back with his objections. It can still become law by a further and more difficult process.

podiatrist, *n* – chiropodist. A new word that takes its place alongside the old.

Podunk, *prop n* – originally an American Indian place name, it now stands for any small and insignificant place: e.g. overheard in a snack bar. 'They gave the job to some jerk from Podunk U because he's got a degree.' First syllable pronounced to rhyme with 'doe'.

poison ivy, *n* – a shrub, indigenous to North America. When touched, the leaves cause a painful skin rash. Also **poison oak** and **poison sumac,** related shrubs with similar effects.

pol, *n* (col) – professional politician. Seen mostly in newsprint.

polecat, *n* – a skunk, or one of several related animals.

police, *v* – to clean and keep clean an outdoor area.

police dog, *n* – an Alsatian. Also called a German shepherd.

policy, *n* – a kind of lottery that used to be conducted illegally in poor city districts.

Pollyanna, *n* – someone characterized by a sunny, everlasting optimism, named after the heroine of a popular sentimental novel of that name published in 1913.

pony, *n* – a crib, a paper from which exam answers are copied.

pony keg, *n* – a small keg of beer, half the normal size.

pony up, *v* – to pay a debt.

pooch, *n* (col) – dog.

poop, *n* (col) – information. A **poop sheet** is a fact sheet.

pooped, *adj* (col) – tired out, exhausted. See also PARTY-POOPER.

pootang, *n* (col) – a black woman considered as a sexual object, or sex with a black woman. Probably from New Orleans and the French *putain* – prostitute.

pop-over, *n* – a thin pastry in the shape of a shell, sometimes with a filling.

popsicle, *n* – a water ice on a stick.

pork barrel, *n* (col) – pertaining to gain from public office, either to enrich the officeholder corruptly, or to enrich his constituents as an inducement to re-elect him.

porpoise, *n* – dolphin.

porterhouse, *n* – a cut of steak

from the part next to the sirloin.

possum, *n* – the common word for an opossum, a marsupial animal indigenous to North America, resembling a large rodent. To **play possum** is to pretend to be asleep or dead, as an opossum does.

post exchange, *n* – see PX.

potato chips, *n* – potato crisps.

potlatch, *n* – a ceremony among some North American West Coast Indians at which the chief gives away things ceremonially, or else burns them, to show that he can afford to. Often used about conspicuous and wasteful consumption.

pot roast, *n* – a dish of meat braised in a casserole.

pound cake, *n* – a rich butter cake, similar to Madeira cake.

powdered sugar, *n* – icing sugar.

practical nurse, *n* – a nurse who does not have full professional qualifications.

prairie schooner, *n* – a romantic term for the covered wagons in which the pioneers travelled Westwards.

precinct, *n* – a district for election and police purposes.

predicate, *v* – to found or base a statement on something, e.g. 'This is predicated on the fact that he's seen the plan and approves it.'

prep school, *n* – a private secondary school and boarding school, with a social cachet, very approximately equivalent to a public school in Britain. **preppy**, as an adjective, is the style of dressing associated with these schools and their social milieu, or as a noun, it means someone who attends such a school.

primary election, *n* – an election in which voters in a state choose the candidate of a particular party from among several nominees. There are Democratic and Republican primaries in some states before the party conventions at which the two presidential candidates are chosen.

prince, *n* (col) – a fine man, praiseworthy fellow.

professor, *n* – a less rarefied post than at a British university, since there are usually several professors to a department. There are also **assistant professors** and **associate professors** who rate the title.

prom, *n* – a dance, usually at a school or university. An abbreviation of 'promenade'.

protest, *v* – protest against. As John Whale pointed out in the *Sunday Times* recently, 'In Britain, convicted men protest their innocence, in America they protest their conviction.'

prowl car, *n* – a police patrol car.

pry, *v* – prise, as in prise open.

psych, *v* – to prepare oneself psychologically for a contest or similar situation.

psyched, psyched up, *adj* – in tune with a situation in a profoundly understanding way. 'Nobody smoked grass there. You were so turned on, so psyched up about what was going on that you didn't need anything.' – student on the 1968 campus rebellion at Columbia University, quoted in

Radical and Militant Youth by Robert Coles.

psych out, *v* – to intimidate indirectly, as by gamesmanship. For instance, if someone about to play a game persuades his opponent that he does not have a chance, he may say, 'I psyched him out at the start.'

public school, *n* – a municipally-run school, the opposite of a private school. In many cities primary schools are called PS —— followed by a number, the initial standing for 'public school'.

pueblo, *n* – an Indian village in the Southwest, or a tribe of Indians who live there.

puke, *v* – to throw up.

Pulitzer prize, *n* – one of several prizes awarded annually for excellence in the arts, letters and journalism, named after the American journalist Joseph Pulitzer.

pull-off, *n* – a lay-by on a motorway.

pumpkin, *n* – an indigenous North American squash, large round, and dull orange in colour.

pumps, *n* – dancing shoes.

punchball, *n* – a kind of street baseball requiring no equipment but a rubber ball, which is punched rather than hit with a bat.

punk, *adj* – trashy, worthless. A **punk** is a low despicable person; tough guy language.

pup tent, *n* – a small low tent for one person.

Purple Heart, *prop n* – a medal awarded to any serviceman wounded in action.

purse, *n* – handbag. A purse (British) is a **change purse**.

pushcart, *n* – barrow.

pussy, *n* (col) – vagina. A lightweight, friendly word for it even though obscene; it has none of the aggressiveness of other synonyms, and is never used as a term of abuse.

put down, *v* – to take down several pegs, to crush, metaphorically. As a noun, it becomes **put-down**, e.g. 'That remark was a put-down.'

PX, *n* (abbr) – post exchange, a shop in a military camp, roughly equivalent to a Naafi.

Q

quart, *n* – 57.8 cubic inches liquid measure, or 67.2 cubic inches dry. A British quart has 69.4 cubic inches.

quarter, *n* – twenty-five cents, a 25-cent coin.

quarterback, *n* – a key position in American football, the man who often carries the ball and decides the next move.

quarterback, *v* – to decide the next move or line to be followed, e.g. 'It is even more true today than it was yesterday that people should not quarterback their own investments.' – Paul A. Samuelson, financial columnist, *Newsweek* magazine.

quarter section, *n* – a track of land one half-mile square.

quick-and-dirty, *n* – a cheap café, or 'caff'.

quirt, *n* – a riding whip of braided leather. Like many words that came out of the old West, this is from the Spanish.

quitter, *n* – someone who gives up easily, who leaves the regiment under fire. 'This is no time for quitters or talk of instant surrender.' – Secretary of State William Rogers on Vietnam.

quonset hut, *n* – a Nissen-type hut.

R

raft, *n* – a large quantity, as in 'A raft of letters was received.' The term dates from the days when a river raft was a major form of goods transport in America, and it meant a raft-full.

rag, *n* and *adj* – to be **on the rag** means to be bad-tempered and irritable. This is an extension of an older meaning, referring to a woman during her menstrual period. To **rag on** somebody means to snap at them irritably and unfairly.

railed, *adj* – drunk.

railroad, *n* – railway.

railway, *n* – a set of tramlines or other rails for a vehicle to travel on, but not a railway in the British sense.

raincheck, *n* – a promise of the same thing at another time instead. When you buy a ticket to an outdoor sporting event in the Northern states, you can also buy, at a small extra cost, a raincheck. This entitles you to another ticket free if the event is postponed because of bad weather. This word is often adapted to other situations.

raise, *n* – a rise in salary. A **rise** to an American often means an erection, so British talk of 'getting a rise' may raise a laugh.

raise, *v* – to rear, bring up. As A.H. Marckwardt observes in his book *American English*: 'In England, farm or garden products are grown, animals are bred and children are reared; in America, all of them are raised.'

raisin bread, *n* – currant bread.

rambunctious, *adj* – riled, uncontrollable, in temperament or mood.

rampike, *n* – a broken or dead tree that still stands.

ranch house or **ranch-type house,** *n* – a long, single storey house with open-plan interior, common in new suburbs.

rap, *n* (col) – talk, chat. This is a modern word, introduced by black Americans through the hip argot.

rare, *adj* – underdone, of meat.

rathskeller, *n* – a place, usually below ground, for festive drinking. A German word.

raunchy, *adj* – crudely sexy.

real estate agent, *n* – estate agent. Also **realtor.** This word was invented in 1915 to give the profession more style, by the Minneapolis Real Estate Board, according to H.L. Mencken.

ream, *v* (col) – to treat someone badly, give a raw deal. Since it also means, to a workman, to widen a hole (there is a tool called a 'reamer') its derivation is clear.

rebel, *n* – a native of the Southern states. The term goes back to the Civil War, when the South rebelled.

receiptor, *n* – in law, a person who holds attached property until litigation ends.

recess, *n* – a break between classes at school, or any other such break.

Reconstruction, *prop n* – the period following the American Civil War in the defeated South. An **unreconstructed Southerner** is one with pre-Civil War attitudes.

redcap, *n* – a railway porter, so called because they traditionally wear red caps with their uniform. A vanishing breed.

red-eye gravy, *n* – a gravy made by adding water to the grease from cooked ham.

redneck, *n* (col) – an ignorant yokel. 'Whatever is wrong with white Southerners – redneck or better – we were all brought up to believe we had a right to think as we pleased.' – from *Scoundrel Time* by Lillian Hellman.

redwood, *n* – the wood of the sequoia tree, much used in furniture. The giant redwood trees in Northern California are among the oldest trees in the world.

reform school, *n* – an approved school, an institution for juvenile law breakers.

regent, *n* – a member of the governing board of a college or university.

regular, *adj* – this also means normal, ordinary; **regular coffee** is coffee with cream and sugar; a **regular guy** is a square, all-round, normal fellow.

relief, *n* – supplementary benefits; welfare payments to someone who is destitute.

relocate, *v* – to move to another town or another country.

remittance man, *n* – someone who lives on cheques sent from home, or remittances.

rent, *v* – hire. One rents furniture, a car, a flat, etc.

reserve bank, *n* – one of the twelve banks attached to the Federal Reserve Bank, the national bank.

rest room, *n* – ladies' or men's room.

résumé, *n* – curriculum vitae.

revenue officer, *n* – an official who enforces the laws against illegal production of liquor. A figure in many folk songs.

review, *v* and *n* – to revise for an exam, or revision.

rib roast, *n* – a joint taken from the forequarter.

ride, *v* – to harass, subject to continual teasing.

ringer, *n* (col) – someone who looks like somebody else. 2. in sport, an illicit substitute, such as a professional who has been infiltrated on to an amateur team.

rinky-dink, *adj* – cheaply made or broken down.

roadster, *n* – a two-seater open sports car.

rock, *n* – 1. a stone. 2. (col) a jewel.

rock and rye, *n* – rye whisky flavoured with a blend of fruits.

rockfish, *n* – striped bass.

rock-ribbed, *adj* (col) — inflexible.

roll, *v* – to rob someone who is drunk or otherwise helpless.

romaine lettuce, *n* – cos lettuce.

rookie, *n* – a new recruit to a calling, used extensively about soldiers, sportsmen and policemen.

roomer, *n* – a lodger. A **rooming house** is a house in which rooms are let.

room-mate, *n* – someone sharing a room, flat or house.

root, *v* – to cheer on, as at a sporting event:

> Root, root, root for the home team.
> If they don't win it's a shame.
>   – from the traditional song 'Take Me Out to the Ball Game'.

root beer, *n* – a soft drink made from roots and herbs, popular with children.

roster, *n* – rota.

roughhouse, *n* – a fight, serious or in fun.

roundhouse, *n* – a wild, hard punch.

roustabout, *n* – an unskilled or semi-skilled labourer, particularly on an oil rig.

rout, *v* – to get someone out of bed.

route, *n* – a delivery round, e.g. **newspaper route.** Pronounced 'rout'. (But curiously, if the word is used as in Britain, it is pronounced as in Britain.)

rowboat, *n* – rowing boat.

rubber, *n* – a condom.

rubber band, *n* – elastic band.

rubberneck, *v* (col) – to go sightseeing, looking this way and that way.

rubbers, *n* — galoshes, overshoes.

rubbing alcohol, *n* – surgical spirit.

rube, *n* – a country bumpkin; short for Reuben, a common country name.

Rube Goldberg, *prop n* – Heath Robinson, i.e. an American cartoonist who drew the same kind of pictures as Robinson, so that 'a Rube Goldberg device' means the same as 'a Heath Robinson device'.

rum, *n* – this often stands for all spirits, as in phrases like 'the demon rum' and 'rum-runners of the Prohibition era'.

rumble, *n* – a street fight, especially between gangs.

rumble seat, *n* – dicky seat.

rummage sale, *n* – jumble sale.

rumpus room, *n* – recreation room.

run, *n* – a ladder in tights or stockings.

run, *v* – to stand for political office.

rush, *v* – on campus, to look for candidates for fraternity or sorority. At universities where these operate, there is often a 'rush week' when pledges (see PLEDGE) are recruited.

rush, *n* – a state of high exhilaration. The word comes from the drug culture, though it does not necessarily refer to drugs.

rutabaga, *n* – a swede.

rye, *n* – whisky made from rye, the commonest kind in the United States.

S

sack, *n* – bed. A masculine word, used typically among the military or on campus. To **sack out** is to go to bed.

sacroiliac, *n* – the base of the spine.

saddle shoes, *n* – leather shoes of two colours.

sad sack, *n* – a blunderer, a loser. Originally an army term.

safe deposit, *n* – a safe place to keep valuables. A **safe deposit box** is a strong box.

sailboat, *n* – sailing boat.

sale, on, *adj* – at reduced price.

sales clerk, *n* – shop assistant.

sales tax, *n* – a tax that is added as a percentage to the purchase price of an article and passed on directly to the customer.

salisbury steak, *n* – chopped steak.

saltine, *n* – a salted cracker, usually served with soup.

salt lick, *n* – a natural salt deposit, a salt flat.

sandbag, *n* – a sack filled with sand used as a weapon.

sandbag, *v* (col) – to knock someone down with a blow from behind, as with a sandbag. Often used metaphorically. 'Lesh decided to sandbag Haig, and sent a courteous letter of rejection to Kissinger.' – from *The Price of Power* by Seymour M. Hersh.

sandbox, *n* – sand pit.

sandlot, *n* – a piece of waste ground in a city where kids play; **sandlot baseball** is a common term.

sanitary napkin, *n* – sanitary towel.

sap, *n* – a cosh.

Saranwrap, *prop n* – a transparent wrapping used mostly for food. Though this is a brand name, it tends to be used for many products of this type.

saratoga trunk, *n* – a large travelling trunk with a rounded top. The term and the object are dated, as is the social position of the resort from which it draws its name, Saratoga Springs.

sarsaparilla, *n* – a soft drink with this flavour.

sashay, *v* (col) – to ambulate, to walk with some style and to some effect.

sasquatch, *n* – a mysterious, much sought-after animal that may or may not exist in the woods of the Northwest. This is an Indian word. The animal is also called **Big Foot**, as the yeti is called the abominable snowman.

sass, *v* – to speak impudently or mockingly. Used with a personal object, e.g. 'In those days rebellion was sassing the cop on the beat.'

sassafras, *n* – a native American tree with aromatic bark and root. These are sometimes used for flavouring.

sauce, *n* – liquor, as in 'He was on the sauce for a while.'

sawbuck, *n* – 1. (col) a 10-dollar bill. 2. a wooden structure that holds something while it is being sawed.

scag, *n* – a low-life, someone or, sometimes, something that is sleazy. **scaggy** is the adjective. 2. heroin.

scallion, *n* – spring onion.

scalper, *n* (col) – a ticket agent who charges an exorbitant commission.

scam, *n* (col) – a nasty cheat.

schlemeil, *n* (col) – a fool or sucker, but seen in terms of endearment. A Yiddish word.

schlock, *n* – junk, or cheap trashy merchandise. Coming from the Yiddish, the word is combined with German to make **schlock-meister**, meaning a manufacturer or purveyor of schlock.

schmaltz, *n* – literally, chicken fat, but it also means anything overladen with sentiment.

schmear, *n* (col) – 1. a bribe, tip or inducement. As a verb, to **schmear** means to bribe someone or simply flatter them in the expectation of favours. 2. situation, thing, as in the phrase 'the whole schmear'.

schmuck, *n* – someone who is stupid and usually nasty.

schnook, *n* (col) – a sucker, fool. It comes from the Yiddish, and like most Yiddish words for a fool, it is affectionate and

pitying. Pronounced to rhyme with 'book'.

schooner, *n* – a large beer glass. Hence, larger than a British schooner.

schtick, *n* – a person's special talent.

scope, *v* – to get information; to check something out. A young people's word.

score, *v* – 1. to attack verbally, criticize sharply. Used mostly in newsprint. 2. (col) to make out with a girl. 3. (col) to succeed in buying some drugs, in the youth argot.

Scotch, *n* – what Americans call Scotch whisky. The word 'whisky' includes rye and bourbon. An American will specify which he wants when ordering.

scow, *n* – a barge for carrying rubbish out to sea.

scratch, *v* – to remove from a list of contenders or candidates.

scratch pad, *n* – notepad.

screen door, *n* – an outer door of mosquito mesh, so that the ordinary inner door can be left open for coolness and insects still be excluded.

screw, *v* – to leave a place, quit.

scrod, *n* – a young Atlantic cod or haddock. A specialty dish in Massachussetts.

scuttlebutt, *n* (col) – rumour, gossip. Originally, a navy term.

scuzzy, *adj* (col) – vile, sleazy, dirty. **scuzz-bag** is a term of abuse formed out of this.

seaboard, *n* – coastline. With reference to the United States, one speaks, for some reason, of the **Eastern seaboard** and the **West coast**, never the 'Western seaboard'.

sea change, *n* – a profound and far-reaching change in a situation.

second guess, *v* – to be wise after the event.

Secret Service, *prop n* – a branch of the Treasury Department that investigates Treasury offences and also has the task of guarding the President and his family. The term does not refer to the CIA.

sedan, *n* – saloon car.

selectman, *n* – in some small towns, an elected member of the town government.

semester, *n* – a term at school.

seminary, *n* – a college for training clergymen of any denomination, not only Roman Catholic, as in Britain.

senior, *n* – a final-year student at high school or university.

set, *v* – (a table) lay a table.

set-up, *n* – water, soda, or other soft drink for mixing with spirits, e.g. 'You bring your own liquor and they make a small charge for set-ups.'

shack up, *v* (col) – to live with someone of the opposite sex out of wedlock.

shad, *n* – a North American deep-bodied herring, a popular food.

shade, *n* – a window blind or awning.

shades, *n* (col) – sunglasses.

shaft, *v* (col) – to treat someone unfairly, usually with deceit.

shag, *v* – to run after, retrieve, or follow. A schoolboy baseball player: 'I practised shagging fly balls.' A detective giving evidence: 'I shagged the suspect right across town.'

shake down, *v* – to extort money.

shakedown cruise, *n* – a sea voyage to try out a newly-commissioned navy ship.

share-cropper, *n* – a tenant farmer who takes as his wage a part of the crop he farms.

shaver, *n* (col) – a boy.

shavetail, *n* – second lieutenant.

shay, *n* – a light, horse-drawn carriage. The word is a corruption of *chaise*.

shebang, *n* (col) – 1. the lot, as in phrases like 'the whole shebang'. 2. a party.

sheenee, *n* (col) – Jew; a racist term, street argot.

shellac, *n* – a high-gloss varnish.

shellacking, *n* – a resounding defeat, a drubbing.

sherbet, *n* – a water ice or sorbet.

shill, *n* – a decoy for a con man.

shim, *n* – a thin strip of metal or wood, used in building.

shine, *n* – 1. a liking, e.g. 'She took a shine to him right away.' 2. (col) a black.

shingle, *n* – a small sign advertising services.

shinny, *v* – to climb vertically a pole or tree by the hands and shins.

shirr, *v* – **shirred eggs** are beaten and then baked; the result is rather like scrambled eggs.

shirtwaist, *n* – woman's blouse.

shoo-in, *n* – an easy victory in an election, a walk-over.

shoot, *v* – 1. send, a racy word, e.g. 'I had a girl friend once, she belonged to this Book of the Month Club. Soon as she'd finished one book, why, they'd shoot her along another.' – from *Picnic* by William Inge.

2. to play certain games; one shoots pool, or craps.

shoot!, *interj* – a common exclamation, rather rural and small townish, clearly a euphemism.

shopping bag, *n* – carrier bag.

short order cook, *n* – a cook who makes simple dishes in the equivalent of a transport café.

short ribs, *n* – a cut from the brisket of beef.

shorts, *n* – underpants, as well as short trousers.

shot, *n* – a measure of spirits.

show, *v* – to come in third in a horse race. An each-way bet in America is a bet on a horse to win, place or show.

showboat, *n* and *v* – a show-off, or, as a verb, to show off.

shower, *n* – a party to give presents to a prospective bride, often of a particular kind, like a **linen shower** or **china shower**. One also has a **baby shower** for a new mother.

Shriner, *n* – a member of the Order of Nobles of the Mystic Shrine, a Masonic-type brotherhood.

shrink, *n* (col) – psychiatrist. Short for 'head-shrinker'.

shuck, *v* – to take off the outer shell or peel.

shyster, *n* – a shifty, dishonest person, usually applied to a lawyer.

sick, *adj* – ill. This word applies to any kind of illness, not only nausea, as in Britain. It was used thus in Shakespeare's British.

sideburns, *n* – sideboards.

side-kick, *n* (col) – one who accompanies and sometimes assists, i.e. Watson to Sherlock Holmes.

sidewalk, *n* – pavement.

sidewheeler, *n* – paddle-steamer.

siding, *n* – a covering on the outside wall of a house.

silk-stocking, *adj* – wealthy, luxurious. The term goes back a long way ('I trust the Gores will find their levees crowded with silk-stocking gentry.' – Thomas Jefferson, writing in his diary, in 1812) and the advent of nylon has not put it out of circulation.

silver, *n* – cutlery, whether silver or not.

Simon Legree, *n* – a harsh taskmaster. Simon Legree was the cruel plantation boss in *Uncle Tom's Cabin*.

sink, *n* – any washbasin, in the bathroom as well as the kitchen.

sinker, *n* (col) – a doughnut (American-style), so-called because it is often dunked in coffee.

skeet shooting, *n* – clay pigeon shooting.

skillet, *n* – frying pan.

skimmer, *n* – a simply-cut dress with straight lines, often sleeveless.

skinny-dip, *n* – nude bathing.

sky pilot, *n* (col) – a service chaplain.

slammer, *n* – jail.

slash, *n* – stroke. 1/2 is spelled out 'one slash two'.

slate, *n* – a list of proposed candidates for office.

sleeper, *n* – a person, event or issue that appears unimportant but turns out to play a key role.

slingshot, *n* – catapult.

slow-poke, *n* – slowcoach.

slug, *n* – a counterfeit coin, such

as might be put into a slot machine.

slugfest, *n* (col) – a fight or, sometimes, a baseball game with a lot of scoring. Derived from the German.

slumgullion, *n* – a meat stew.

slush, *n* – a crushed-ice drink.

slush fund, *n* – a fund set aside for secret, often corrupt, payments.

smackers, *n* (col) – dollars, used only in the plural. One might say 'a hundred smackers', but never 'a smacker'.

smart, *adj* – clever. In school, at least, a term of approval.

smart ass, *n* and *adj* (col) – smart alec.

smarts, *n* (col) – brains, nous.

smidgen, *n* – a small amount.

smoke-filled room, *n* – a back room at a political gathering where deals are hatched in private. The term came into use during the Republican Party convention of 1920, in a description of the process by which Warren Harding was nominated; it is credited to Kirk Simpson, an Associated Press reporter, and has now found its way into the dictionaries.

smoker, *n* – an informal social gathering for men only. The term is dated, and goes back to the days when men did not smoke in front of ladies.

smokestack, *n* – chimney or funnel.

smokey, *n* (col) – a highway patrolman. A word from CB radio.

smudge, *n* – a smoky fire, usually lit to drive away insects, or give a signal.

snafu, *n* (col) – a cock-up. Originally a service term, it is an acronym of 'situation normal, all fouled-up' (in its politer version).

snake, *v* – to steal someone else's girl friend or boy friend. A young people's term.

snake fence, *n* – a zig-zag fence made of horizontal rails coming together at an angle.

snap-brim, *n* and *adj* – a felt hat with a brim turned down in front and up at the back.

snatch, *n* (col) – vagina. Mildly obscene. When I was broadcasting from Northern Ireland for an American radio service, I spoke once about British Army snatch squads active on the streets at night, which provoked some merriment at the other end. The term is used less than it was in my college days.

sneaker, *n* – gym shoe.

snow, *v* (col) – to talk deceptively but soothingly. 'What a technique that guy has. He'd start snowing his date in this very quiet, sincere voice – like as if he wasn't only a very handsome guy but a nice, sincere guy, too.' – from *The Catcher in the Rye* by J.D. Salinger.

snow job, *n* (col) – a cover-up, a whitewash story.

socialite, *n* – someone who is distinguished for his or her social life and nothing else.

social register, *n* – a book detailing who's who in the social élite.

social security, *n* – old age pension, or the system of paying for and receiving old age pensions.

sock hop, *n* – an informal dance, typically an undergraduate event, at which people take off their shoes to dance.

soda or **soda pop,** *n* – any carbonated soft drink. Distinguished from soda water by the use of an article, e.g. 'Let's have a soda.'

soda cracker, *n* – a plain biscuit leavened with bicarbonate of soda, usually eaten with butter.

soda jerk, *n* (col) – see JERK.

softball, *n* – a game similar to baseball, but played with a larger, softer ball and ten to a side instead of nine. It is played mostly by youngsters; there is no professional softball.

solicitor, *n* – 1. a legal officer of a city or a town. 2. a fund raiser.

solitaire, *n* – the game of patience.

solon, *n* – a legislator. The word comes from the name of the great law-maker of ancient Athens. Seen only in newsprint.

sophomore, *n* – a student in the second year of his or her four-year course in secondary school or university. The word is itself a comment on that stage of life, in that it comes from the Greek words *sophos*, wise, and *moros*, foolish.

sorehead, *n* – a disgruntled or unjustly complaining person; a poor loser.

sorghum, *n* – a cane-like grass with a sweet-tasting juice, or a kind of dark treacle made from the juice, traditionally Southern.

sorority, *n* – on campus, the female equivalent of fraternity. See FRATERNITY.

soul, *n* – an aspect of the black American spirit, involving direct access to basic emotions, free expression and racial pride. Much used in combination, as **soul brother, soul food** and **soul music.**

southpaw, *n* – someone who is left-handed. Originally a baseball term.

sowbelly, *n* – bacon. A Western term.

spaced out, *adj* – high, usually on drugs, on Cloud Nine. **spacy** is a milder version; a youngster who says he is feeling spacy means only that he is feeling vague and not quite with it. A **space cadet** is someone who is out of touch with reality and *lives* on Cloud Nine.

speakeasy, *n* – an illegal drinking place during the Prohibition years.

special delivery, *adj* – express. A postal term.

speedway, *n* – motorway.

speed zone, *n* – a zone in which the driving speed is restricted.

spic, *n* (col) – a Latin or Latin-American. A racist term.

spiel, *n* – a line of talk, particularly high-pressure sales talk. A **spieler** is someone whose stock-in-trade this is.

spigot, *n* – a small tap on a barrel or a tank. In Britain, this means only the winding part of the tap.

spike, *v* (col) – to add liquor to a non-alcoholic drink. In high schools, there is traditionally an attempt by students to spike the lemonade punch at the school dance.

spike heels, *n* – stiletto heels.

spitball, *n* – 1. a pellet made of

chewed paper, as thrown by schoolboys. 2. in baseball, a ball with spit rubbed into one side which supposedly can make it curve in flight.

splitsville, *n* (col) – 'They're in splitsville,' means they are splitting, i.e. getting a divorce.

spook, *n* (col) – 1. CIA man. 2. a black; a racist term.

spool, *n* – reel of cotton, wire, tape, etc.

sporting house, *n* – brothel.

square knot, *n* – reef knot.

squash, *n* – a genus of fruits, eaten as vegetables, that includes the marrow. The word is seen on American menus.

stag, *adj* (col) – without a girl partner at a social event; **going stag** to a dance means without a girl. ' "Chutzpah" is going stag to a wife-swapping party.' – contemporary joke.

standby, *n* – understudy.

standing, *n* – on a street sign, it means parking. 'No standing' means 'No parking'.

stand-upper, *n* – a piece spoken directly into a television camera, what in British TV is called an on-camera.

Stars and Bars, *prop n* – the flag of the Confederacy.

state, *adj* – pertaining to state, as opposed to Federal, authority. In a political context, it sometimes means the opposite of what it would mean in Britain. For instance, a campaign for more state control of education would be a campaign *against* central control.

statehouse, *n* – the building which houses a state legislature.

state's evidence, *n* – evidence for the prosecution in a criminal case.

state trooper, *n* – a state policeman.

state university, *n* – the university which every state has and supports, tuition being low-cost to residents of that state.

station, *n* – extension, on a telephone. One might dial a number and ask for 'station 1304'.

station wagon, *n* – estate car.

statutory rape, *n* – sexual intercourse with a girl under the age of consent.

steamer, *n* – 1. in the kitchen, a poacher. 2. a clam, cooked usually by steaming.

steer, *n* – a castrated bull or ox. **bum steer,** *n* (col) – a bad tip, bad advice.

stenographer, *n* – shorthand typist.

stickball, *n* – a crude version of baseball played in city streets.

stick pin, *n* – tie-pin.

stiff, *v* – to avoid tipping. 'Some tenants stiff you completely.' – porter in a block of flats, quoted in the *New Yorker*.

stir, *n* (col) – jail.

stockade, *n* – military prison.

stock company, *n* – repertory company. **summer stock** is a repertory company that works only in the summer holiday season, as many do.

stockyard, *n* – cattle yard.

stogey or **stogie,** *n* (col) – a cheap cigar. First syllable pronounced to rhyme with 'toe', the scond with a hard 'g'.

stomp, *n* – a stomping dance done to jazz music.

stomp, *v* (col) – to stamp on

someone when he's on the ground.

stool pigeon, *n* (col) – an informer.

stoop, *n* – a porch separated from the street by several steps, seen on terraced houses in many American cities. The word comes from the Dutch *stoep*, and originated in New York when it was the Dutch colony of New Amsterdam.

store, *n* – any shop. 'Here's the grocery store and here's Mr Morgan's drugstore. Most everybody in town manages to look into those two stores once a day.' – from *Our Town* by Thornton Wilder. A **store clerk** is a shop assistant.

storm cellar, *n* – a cellar with an entrance outside the house where refuge can be taken in severe storms.

storm door, *n* – a second door in front of the first for extra protection from fierce storms. Also **storm window**.

stovepipe hat, *n* (col) – top hat.

straight, *n* – of a drink, neat, e.g. 'straight whisky'. **straight-up** means without ice.

straight-arrow, *adj* – absolutely honest and straightforward.

strawberry blonde, *n* – a girl with reddish-blonde hair.

strawberry shortcake, *n* – a shortcake topped with strawberries and whipped cream.

straw boss, *n* – a subordinate boss; charge hand.

straw poll, *n* – an informal poll of opinion.

streetcar, *n* – tram, as in *A Streetcar Named Desire*. The word 'tram' is unknown in America.

street lamp, *n* – lamp-post.

street light, *n* – street lamp.

strict constructionist, *n* – someone who interprets the American Constitution narrowly. Members of the Supreme Court and other national jurists are often divided into strict and **loose constructionists**,

strike, *n* – a baseball term. A batter is out when he has three strikes against him. The term is adapted to many situations; the meaning of 'He had two strikes against him from the start,' for instance, is clear. To **strike out** means to fail.

stringer, *n* – a timber spanning a railway trestle or bridge.

stroke, *v* – to talk to someone simply so as to enhance their self-esteem rather than to convey information. From the analogy of stroking a dog.

stroller, *n* – an infant's pushchair.

stumblebum, *n* (col) – a hopeless fool.

stump, *v* – to go on a political campaign, e.g. 'He stumped New England for Reagan.'

stump orator, *n* – a rabble-rouser.

submarine sandwich, *n* – another term for **hero sandwich**, a section of French loaf with a lot of filling.

substitute teacher, *n* – supply teacher.

subway, *n* – tube train.

succotash, *n* – a mixture of green corn and beans; a popular vegetable dish, it is indigenous, as is the word, which comes from a similar Iroquois Indian word.

suck, *v* (col) – to be a failure,

unpleasant, dislikeable. 'It sucks!' means 'It stinks!'

sucker, *n* – it also means a lollipop. An **all-day sucker** is a huge one.

suds, *n* – beer. Hard-hat talk (see HARD-HAT).

summation, *n* – a lawyer's closing speech in a court case.

summer soldier, *n* – someone who supports a cause only when the going is easy. The phrase is Thomas Paine's; in the darkest days of the American War of Independence, when many were deserting the cause, he wrote scornfully, in *The American Crisis,* of 'the summer soldier and the sunshine patriot'.

sunny side up, *adj* – used about fried eggs, this means fried on one side only so that the liquid yolk beams upwards. The alternative method of frying is on both sides, or **over,** so that the yolk is concealed between layers of white.

super, *n* – the superintendent of a block of flats. Nearly every block has one.

superhighway, *n* – motorway.

surrey, *n* – a light, four-wheeled, horse-drawn carriage.

suspenders, *n* – braces.

sweat, *n* (col) – trouble, effort, used mostly in the negative phrase **no sweat,** meaning 'It's no trouble.'

sweet potato, *n* – 1. a vegetable only distantly related to the potato, eaten widely instead of potatoes in the United States. It is indigenous to America as, indeed, was the potato originally. Among sweet potato-eating people, ordinary potatoes are called white potatoes. 2. an ocarina, a musical instrument.

swinger, *n* – as well as its original meaning, a lively with-it person, it also means someone who goes in for wife-swapping. A famous book of folk music is called *I Hear America Singing* and Peter de Vries called his comic novel about contemporary sex mores *I Hear America Swinging.*

swing shift, *n* – an evening shift at work.

switch, *n* – a point on a railway.

switchblade, *n* – a flick-knife.

switch hitter, *n* (col) – a baseball term meaning someone who can bat left- or right-handed, it now also means someone who is bisexual.

syndicate, *n* – a highly organized crime ring.

T

T, model, *n* – see MODEL T.

tab, *n* – bill.

table, *v* – to set aside a motion rather than discuss it. This is the exact opposite of the meaning in Britain. (See TABLE in the British/American section.)

table cream, *n* – single cream.

tack or **thumb tack,** *n* – drawing pin.

tacky, *adj* – shabby, somewhat on the seedy side. The word has a small-townish flavour, e.g. the oft-quoted verdict of the *Kansas City Star* (2 December 1931): 'English women have the knack of looking tacky even when they are wealthy and titled.' It also now can mean vulgar or cheap – shabby in the metaphorical sense – as in 'That was a tacky thing to do.'

taco, *n* – a Mexican dish, a sort of crispy pancake with a meat and cheese filling, often eaten as a snack, particularly in the West.

tad, *n* – a very small amount, or a small boy.

taffy, *n* – toffee.

tailgate, *n* – the tailboard of a van or lorry.

tailgate, *v* – to drive very closely behind another vehicle.

take down, *v* – to take up a loan, i.e. to draw the money.

take-out, *adj* – take-away, e.g. a 'take-out Chinese restaurant'.

tamale, *n* – a Mexican dish popular in America, made of crushed corn, meat and red pepper.

Tammany Hall, *prop n* – the headquarters of the political machine that ran New York City politics for a long time, often used to signify boss-ruled or corrupt municipal politics.

tan, *v* (col) – to smack, as in 'I'll tan his hide.'

tank, *n* (col) – a cell in which prisoners are held pending further investigation or trial.

tar baby, *n* – something you get into, voluntarily to start with, then get stuck in and cannot get out of. Thus, it was said that 'Vietnam was LBJ's tar baby.' The term comes from one of the Uncle Remus children's stories, in which a doll is made out of tar so that Brer Rabbit will shake hands with it and get stuck.

tardy, *adj* – late. Used much in schools.

tart, *n* – tartlet.

taxi dancer, *n* – a girl who works in a dance hall and dances with customers for a price for each dance. Dates back to the hey-day of the dance hall, though rarely seen today.

tea cart, *n* – tea trolley.

teamster, *n* – a vehicle-driver. The term dates back to the days when he drove a team of horses, and now it is used almost only in the collective, about the 'teamsters' as a labour force.

teed off, *adj* – cheesed off.

teeter totter, *n* – a see-saw.

teleprompter, *n* – autocue. A trade name that has come to stand for the object.

teletypewriter, *n* – teleprinter.

temple, *n* – a synagogue other than an orthodox one.

tenderloin, *n* – 1. a fillet steak. 2. the **tenderloin district** is the night club and brothel section of a town.

> Some write back home to the old folks for coin,
> That's their ace in the hole.
> And some got a gal in the old tenderloin,
> That's their ace in the hole.
> – traditional jazz song.

tennies, *n* – tennis shoes, or plimsolls.

tenure, *n* – in the academic world, permanency of appointment.

termite, *n* – a wood-eating white ant.

territory, *n* – an area under US Government jurisdiction, usually with a certain amount of self-government, which does not have statehood. The Virgin Islands are a territory; most states were territories before they were admitted to the Union.

terrycloth, *n* – a pile-fabric, usually a bath towel, with loops at the side so that it can be draped around the body.

Thanksgiving, *prop n* – a national holiday, the fourth Thursday in November, traditionally a time of family reunions and fireside celebrations. It marks the end of gathering in the first harvests by the Pilgrim Fathers at Plymouth, Massachusetts, in 1621. A ritual Thanksgiving Dinner includes turkey and pumpkin pie.

theme, *n* – a schoolboy's or schoolgirl's essay.

Thirteen Colonies, *prop n* – the original American colonies which rebelled against British rule.

thirty, *n* – signifying the end of a newspaper story. In the early days of the telegraph, operators would put XXX at the end of a dispatch to a newspaper; this was read as Roman numerals and became thirty.

thread, *n* – cotton.

threads, *n* (col) – clothes. Used mostly by young people.

through, *conj* – 1. on the telephone, this means finished, not connected. If you tell an American telephone operator that you're through, she's likely to cut you off. 2. in time, until the end, e.g. 'through July' means until 31 July.

throughway, *n* – a motorway.

ticket, *n* – a list of candidates put forward by a party.

tic tac toe, *n* – noughts and crosses.

tie, *n* – a railway sleeper.

tights, *n* – ballet tights or similar. What in Britain are called tights are **hose** or **pantyhose**.

tightwad, n (col) – a miserly person. It means he holds his wad of notes tightly.

timber line, n – the line in a mountainous or cold region beyond which trees do not grow.

tinhorn, n (col) – a loud-mouthed boaster making fraudulent claims, often used about gamblers.

tinkle, n – pee. A childish term.

together, adj – organized, integrated. Someone may be described as 'a together person'.

tokenism, n – a policy that has the appearance of social change but is merely cosmetic; for instance, promoting one black to a very visible executive position as a 'token' of racial integration.

Tom, n – short for **Uncle Tom**. From *Uncle Tom's Cabin*, it means a black who strives to earn the good opinion of whites, and is a term of disdain.

Tom Collins, n – a long iced drink of gin, lemon juice, soda and sugar, popular in the summertime.

ton, n – 2,000 lb, a 'short ton' in Britain.

tongue depressor, n – a doctor's spatula.

Tony, prop n – the Antoinette Perry awards for excellence in the Broadway theatre, awarded annually. The theatre's equivalent of the Oscar.

tony, adj (col) – high-toned.

toque, n – a small, woollen hat.

torch singer, n – a female singer, who sings popular songs in a romantic, moody, usually sad vein.

tortilla, n – a thin pancake made from corn meal. A Mexican dish popular in America.

Tory, n – historically, one who remained loyal to Britain during the American War of Independence.

total, v – to wreck totally, usually a car.

tote, v – to carry a heavy burden, as in 'tote dat barge, lift dat bale . . .' from the song 'Ol' Man River'.

touchdown, n – the scoring play in American football.

touch football, n – a mock-football (American), played by any number of people, in which a touch is substituted for a tackle.

town meeting, n – a meeting of all the citizens of a village or small town, or else the qualified voters, to discuss and decide community issues.

track, n – 1. athletics, as in **track team** and **track meetings**. 2. racecourse.

tracking, v part – streaming in schools.

track-layer, n – a plate-layer on the railway.

track home, n – one of a row of houses in a street that are all the same.

trade, v – swap. Much used by children.

trade-off, n – an exchange of one concession or gain for another. Commonly used in modern discussion of international or business strategy.

traffic circle, n – roundabout.

trailer, n – caravan.

tramp, *n* (col) – a near-prostitute, a scrubber. A very insulting term. It has come into use since that song of the early 1940s, 'The Lady Is a Tramp'; then it simply meant that the lady was gaily unconventional.

transom, *n* – fanlight.

trash, *n* – rubbish. A **trash can** is a dustbin.

trash, *v* (col) – to wreck, vandalize; a word from hippy argot.

trick, *n* – a turn by a prostitute.

trick or treat, *n* – the traditional children's cry to a householder on Hallowe'en, meaning that unless they are given a present, usually sweets, they will carry out some destructive prank.

trimming, *n* – defeat.

Trojan, *prop n* – the most common brand of condom.

trolley, *n* – tram.

truck, *n* – 1. a lorry, or wagon. A **fire truck** is a fire engine. 2. vegetables raised for the market. 3. a kind of dragging, distracted walk, a word from the drug culture.

trucker, *n* – 1. market gardener. 2. lorry-driver.

truck stop, *n* – transport café.

trunk, *n* – the boot of a car.

t.s., *n* (abbr, col) – hard cheese; actually, an abbreviation of

'tough shit'. *Stars and Stripes*, the US Army newspaper, in a series of useful phrases for GIs stationed in France, once gave it as a translation of *C'est la guerre*.

tube, *n* – 1. valve, as in a radio or television set. 2. television. The American equivalent of Britain's 'the box'. Also called the **boob tube**.

tuckered or **tuckered-out**, *adj* – tired out, exhausted.

turkey, *n* – a loser. In the theatre, it means specifically a flop.

turnover, *n* – a filled pastry, like a tart, made by turning one half of the crust over the other.

turnpike, *n* – a road with toll gates.

turtleneck, *n* – polo neck.

tuxedo, *n* – a dinner jacket or dinner suit.

twirler, *n* – a drum majorette, who twirls the baton.

twister, *n* – tornado.

two bits, *n* – 25 cents (see also BIT); **two-bit**, *adj* (col) means small-time, of little worth.

two-fers, *n* – theatre tickets sold two for the price of one, when a theatre has plenty of empty seats.

U

uncle, *n* – saying 'uncle' is a token of surrender. 'Uncle Sam isn't about to say "uncle",' was one of President Ford's pronouncements on the energy crisis.

Uncle Tom, *n* – see TOM.

underground railroad, *n* – before the American Civil War, a chain of people who helped runaway slaves, passing them along from one hiding place to another until they reached the Canadian border and safety.

undershirt, *n* – vest. A 'vest' in American is a waistcoat.

unglued, *adj* (col) – crazy, or simply out of control, going to pieces.

unit rule, *n* – a rule whereby, at a political convention, a majority of delegates of one state cast the entire vote of that delegation.

upchuck, *v* – vomit. A variation of **chuck up**.

up front, *adj* – 1. open for all to see. 2. talking about money, it means paid in advance.

upgrade, *adj* – uphill; **on the upgrade** means improving, getting better.

upset price, *n* – reserve price, as at an auction.

uptown, *n* and *adj* – away from the centre of the city and usually in the more residential areas; as a direction, it is the opposite of downtown (see DOWNTOWN).

V

vacuum bottle or **vacuum flask,** *n* – thermos flask.

valedictorian, *n* – the student who delivers the so-called valedictory oration at the graduation ceremony. This is an honour.

vamoose, *v* (col) – scram. It comes from the Spanish.

vaudeville, *n* – music-hall.

veep, *n* (col) – the Vice-President, a contraction of VP.

venire, *n* – a panel from which a jury is chosen.

vest, *n* – waistcoat.

vest pocket, *adj* – designed to fit into a waistcoat pocket, hence miniature.

veteran, *n* – an ex-serviceman of any age.

Veterans' Day, *prop n* – Remembrance Sunday.

Victor Charlie, *prop n* (col) – the Vietcong, from the initials VC. A Vietnam War army term that has become widely known. Sometimes abbreviated to **Charlie.**

victrola, *n* – record-player. The original term when the instrument was invented, it is somewhat antiquated now, but still used.

visiting fireman, *n* – a visitor from out of town, particularly someone come to see the big city.

Volstead Act, *n* – the law forbidding the sale of alcoholic beverage that brought in Prohibition. Also **Volstead Era** – the Prohibition years.

W

WAC, *prop n* (abbr) – Women's Army Corps.

WAF, *prop n* (abbr) – Women in the Air Force, equivalent of the WRAF.

waldorf salad, *n* – a salad made up principally of diced apples, celery, nuts and mayonnaise.

walking papers, *n* (col) – the sack from a job, or forced departure of any kind. If a girl breaks off a romance, it may be said that she 'gave him his walking papers'.

walk-up, *n* – a flat or room on the upper storey of a building that has no lift.

walkway, *n* – pedestrian way.

walleye, *n* – pike-perch.

wall-eyed, *adj* – having eyes pointed apart. The opposite of cross-eyed.

Wall Street, *prop n* – the New York financial world; the term is the equivalent of 'the City'. It is actually the main street in the financial district of New York.

wampum, *n* – Indian bead money. A childish colloquialism for 'money'.

warden, *n* – the governor of a prison.

ward-heeler, *n* – a minor official of a political party who performs small duties on a local, i.e. ward, level.

warming oven, *n* – hot drawer.

wash cloth, *n* – flannel, a word unknown in America.

wash up, *v* – to wash oneself, not the dishes. Philip French recalled in a *New Statesman* article that he once suggested to his American hostess that he help her wash up, and was met with a startled look.

WASP, *n* – an acronym for White Anglo-Saxon Protestant, the dominant ethnic group in the United States. Professor Robert Burchfield, in a BBC radio discussion on American and British speech (8 August 1983), let slip a remark about 'Waspish Americans', and was widely misunderstood.

Wasserman test, *n* – the standard test for syphilis. In some states, it is compulsory before marriage.

waste, *v* – to kill (a Vietnam War word) or, by extension, to beat decisively in a game or contest.

water cooler, *n* – a machine that keeps and dispenses cold drinking water, usually along with paper cups. Most offices in America have one.

water tower, *n* – a tower, raised above the ground, that serves as a reservoir for small towns.

wax paper, *n* – greaseproof paper.

way, *adj* – very or very far, as in 'It's way over that way.' **way back,** *n* – a long time ago.

wedding band, *n* – wedding ring.

weenie, *n* – a hot dog. A corruption of Vienna (Wiener) sausage.

West Point, *prop n* – the location of the US Military Academy, and the common name for the Academy; equivalent of Sandhurst.

wet-back, *n* (col) – an illegal immigrant. The term comes from the Southwest, where the Mexicans used to swim across the Rio Grande to enter the United States illegally.

whammy, *n* (col) – malevolent feeling, with a hint of supernatural powers. 'Green's got the whammy on me. They've got the whammy on each other, and nothing can change the whammy that springs up between one person and another and usually lasts a lifetime.' – from *Something Happened* by Joseph Heller.

whipoorwill, *n* – a nocturnal bird with an insistent call. Until a few years ago, it was a feature of the Southern states, but has now migrated in large numbers to New England.

whipping cream, *n* – double cream.

whistlestop, *v* – to travel about the country by train on a political campaign.

whistlestop town, *n* – a small, unimportant town, so-called because the train only stops there when signalled by a whistle.

white lightning, *n* – crude, fierce, home-made whisky.

wholewheat, *n* – wholemeal.

whomping, *adj* – enormous, usually in a metaphorical sense rather than as physical description, e.g. 'a whomping increase of $150 a week'.

wild, *adj* (col) – in addition to its literal meaning, this means far-out, fantastic. Two examples heard in conversation: a traveller returned from the Far East: 'We got into some wild situations.' Someone talking about a girl: 'She's got a wild build!'

wildcat strike, *n* – unofficial strike.

windbreaker, *n* – windcheater.

window shade, *n* – blind or awning.

windshield, *n* – windscreen.

Windy City, *prop n* – Chicago.

wing dam, *n* – a barrier to protect a river bank from erosion by a fast current.

wire, *n* – telegram.

wire service, *n* – a news agency that distributes its news by teleprinter, like Reuter and the Associated Press.

wobbly, *n* (col) – a member of the IWW, the Industrial Workers of the World, a radical movement in the early years of this century, whose most famous martyr was Joe Hill.

wood alcohol, *n* – methylated spirits.

woodchuck, *n* – a thick-set marmot, a furry bushy-tailed rodent, 2–3 feet long.

wood trim, *n* – woodwork in a house.

wop, *n* (col) – an insulting term for an Italian-American.

work-out, *n* – bout of strenuous exercise.

work over, *v* (col) – to beat up systematically.

World Series, *prop n* – the climax of the baseball season, at the end of the summer, a series of up to seven games between the champions of the two leagues.

wrangler, *n* – a cowboy who breaks in wild horses.

wrap, *n* – a woman's coat or other outer garment.

write-in, *v* – to vote for a candidate whose name is not on the ballot paper by writing it on. Also used as a noun.

Y

Y, *prop n* (abbr) – the YMCA or YWCA, or usually the hostel that these organizations run in most big cities. Used in phrases like 'staying at the Y'.

yam, *n* – sweet potato (see SWEET POTATO), and some related tuberous vegetables.

Yankee, *n* – among most Americans, a native of one of the New England states. Among Southerners, any Northerner. An Englishman I met once was travelling back through the United States from Mexico, and was entertained by some people in Tennessee. Talking about business in Mexico, he remarked that there was a lot of Yankee money and enterprise down there. There was a cool silence after this, and then someone said resentfully, 'Well, I'll bet there's some rebel money and rebel enterprise down there too.'

yard, *n* – any area around a home, whether it is carpeted with concrete, grass or flowers. Most English front or back gardens would be called 'yards' in America. The word 'garden' is usually used only if it is cultivated with special, almost professional, care, or is used for growing vegetables.

yardbird, *n* – convict. Charlie 'Bird' Parker, the great alto saxophonist, was given his nickname because he had spent some time in prison.

yegg, *n* – a professional thief. According to the *Dictionary of American Slang*, the word comes from the name of John Yegg, whom it says was the first safe-cracker to use nitroglycerine.

yellow jack, *n* – yellow fever. Also, at sea, this means the yellow flag raised on a ship to indicate that there is a contagious disease on board.

yenta, *n* – a gossip, a person who talks continually, particularly a woman. From the Yiddish. A piece of literary graffiti in a men's room off Harvard Square read recently: 'Proust was a yenta.'

you-all, *pron* – 'you' in the South. Its use is popularly taken as the mark of a Southerner. Non-Southerners doing a comic imitation always use this in addressing an individual, but most Southerners insist that it is used only in the plural. As H.L. Mencken remarks in a short dissertation on this word, the subject is fraught with bitterness.

yo-yo, *n* – a stupid or zany person.

Z

zaftig or **zoftig**, *adj* – having a luscious, rounded figure. From a Yiddish word *zaftig*, that means, literally, juicy.

zap, *v* (col) – hit, knock down, kill.

zee, *n* – zed, the last letter of the alphabet.

zilch, *n* (col) – nothing, zero.

zinger, *n* – something that lands right on the target, usually to uncomfortable effect, such as a question that strikes at the vitals and is difficult to answer.

zip code, *n* – postal code.

zip gun, *n* – a home-made gun that fires a bullet by means of a spring.

zonked, *adj* (col) – 1. stoned, high on drugs. 2. struck, knocked-out, usually metaphorically.

zucchini, *n* – courgette. Pronounced 'zookeenee'.

ALSO . . .

American

British

British/American

A

access television, *n* – television air time allocated for use by outside, independent groups.

accommodation address, *n* – a forwarding address that usually conceals one's identity, like a box number.

account, *n* – 1. a bill, usually one sent regularly for services or several purchases. 2. charge account.

accumulator, *n* – 1. a storage battery, as in a car. 2. in horse-racing, a parlay, a combination of bets in which the winnings on one, if any, are staked on the next race.

ackers, *n* (col) – money.

adventure playground, *n* – a children's playground with equipment for adventurous play, such as a tree house and a wagon run. A common feature of city parks.

advert, *n* – short for advertisement. The American equivalent is 'ad'.

aerial, *n* – antennae.

afters, *n* – dessert. Used mostly by or to children.

aggro, *n* (col) – rough stuff, fighting. A newish term; street gang language. It comes from 'aggravation'.

aircraftman, *n* – an RAF rank equivalent to airman.

airing cupboard, *n* – a closet built around a hot water pipe or tank, so that newly-washed clothes can be warmed there.

air marshal, *n* – an RAF rank equivalent to general. There are also air vice marshals below and air chief marshals above.

airscrew, *n* – propeller. This is the term used within the aviation industry; outside it, people say 'propeller'.

airship, *n* – dirigible.

airy-fairy, *adj* (col) – fanciful, head-in-the-clouds.

alderman, *n* – in Britain, these were senior members of a borough or town council, chosen from among and by the councillors. The office was abolished in 1974.

A-levels, *n* – an important exam taken at college entrance level, usually in three subjects.

Alf Garnett, *prop n* – British television's equivalent of Archie Bunker, or a person holding those views. Actually, since Alf Garnett was the original model, it would be more correct to say that Archie Bunker is America's Alf Garnett.

all, *comb adj* (col) – used following certain other words, it means emphatically, 'absolutely nothing', as in the common phrases **damn-all, bugger-all**

and **sod-all**; these last two are rather vulgar. The mythical Welsh village in which Dylan Thomas set his poetic play *Under Milk Wood* is called Llareggub (many Welsh names begin with a double 'l'). This was a joke on the British Broadcasting Corporation, which first commissioned it; the name is 'bugger-all' spelled backwards.

Alliance, *prop n* – in politics, the electoral alliance between the Liberal and Social Democratic parties (see LIBERAL PARTY and SOCIAL DEMOCRATIC PARTY).

all-in, *adj* – 1. exhausted, of a person. 2. all-inclusive, used of a service. If a holiday hotel rate is all-in, it means that it includes food, service, etc.

allotment, *n* – a small plot rented out for growing vegetables and flowers. Many city-dwellers grow vegetables on allotments.

almoner, *n* – the old term for a social worker in a hospital.

Alsatian, *n* – German shepherd dog.

anglepoise lamp, *n* – an adjustable desk lamp with a long arm. Originally a trade name.

Anglo-Catholic, *prop adj* – High Church Anglican (see HIGH CHURCH).

anorak, *n* – parka.

Antipodes, the, *prop n* – Australia and New Zealand.

approved school, *n* – a reform school for boys or girls up to the age of sixteen. Now officially called a 'community home'.

apropos, *adj* – relevant. It can also be used as an adverb to begin a sentence as a substitute for 'talking about . . .' as in 'apropos my Aunt Matilda . . .'

argy-bargy, *n* (col) – argument.

arse, *n* – ass, in the anatomical sense; fanny. **arse over tit** (col) means head over heels in a fall (or as, allegedly, more educated people might say, 'base over apex').

articled, *adj* – appointed a lawyer-in-training in a legal office.

articulated, *adj* – made up of several different parts. An **articulated lorry** is a trailer truck.

artiste, *n* – a stage performer. The word is used for a member of a ballet troupe, and apart from that, mostly for people on the outer fringes of the profession, with misplaced pretentiousness. Vaudeville performers and strippers are often called 'artistes', but not someone acting in a play on the London stage.

ass, *n* – a fool, particularly someone whose foolishness is very evident. The term is less rude than in America because it does not mean a part of the anatomy, but a donkey (the other is **arse** – see above). The difference is illustrated thus by Ashley Montagu in *The Anatomy of Swearing*:

> There was a young woman
>   named Glass
> Who had a most beautiful ass,
> Not rounded and pink
> As you probably think,
> But was grey, and had ears,
>   and ate grass.

assessor, *n* – a claims adjuster in insurance.

assurance, *n* – life insurance.

athletics team, *n* – track team.

aubergine, *n* – eggplant.

aunt sally, *n* – something set up in order to be knocked down – an argument, for instance – or an easy target for attack.

autocue, *n* – equivalent to a Teleprompter.

Aye aye, *interj* – a phrase that means 'There's more to this than meets the eye,' and points to some further, usually murky significance. It could be a rejoinder to 'He seems to have a lot of money all of a sudden,' or 'I have to meet a lady for a private discussion.'

B

back benches, *n* – the benches in the House of Commons where the rank and file members sit. Members of the government and the shadow cabinet sit across the floor from each other on the front benches. A **back bencher** is a rank-and-file Member of Parliament. See FRONT BENCH.

back-hander, *n* (col) – payment on the side, usually illicit.

backlog, *n* – this stands for the same thing as in American but points in a different direction, like a number with a minus sign in front of it instead of a plus sign. In Britain it means a pile-up of something that cannot easily be cleared, and has implications of a log-jam. A businessman might say woefully, 'I've got a backlog of work,' as an apology for late delivery.

back passage, *n* – the rectal passage.

back-to-back, *n* – small houses built in rows, joined at the back. Found in the poorer parts of industrial towns, usually built in the last century.

bag, *n* – the amount of game killed or caught in a day.

bag, *v* – to catch or kill, usually in hunting. In schoolboy language, to claim something.

bags, *n* (col) – 1. lots. There is

no singular use in this sense. 2. trousers. Rather old-fashioned.

bailiff, *n* – as well as a court official, this also means the manager of an estate or farm.

bairn, *n* – infant. Mostly Scottish and North country.

bakshee, *n* (col) – free. From the Arab beggar's plea for 'baksheesh', brought back by the army from the Middle East. Often pronounced and occasionally spelled 'bukshee'.

balaclava, *n* – a warm woollen headgear that covers the ears, first worn by soldiers at Balaclava during the Crimean War.

ballocks, *n* – a variation of **bollocks** (see).

balls-up, *n* (col) – snafu, fouled-up situation.

banbury cake, *n* – a kind of mince pie.

banger, *n* (col) – 1. an old car, a clunker, equally onomatopoeic. 2. a sausage.

bang-on, *adj* (col) – on the button; just what's needed. Not surprisingly, the term originated with Second World War bomber crews.

bank holiday, *n* – a national holiday, i.e. a day on which the banks are closed. One Rev. Gerald Smeaton wrote to the London *Times* on April 2, 1976 to complain of this terminology, which puts the role of the banks at the center of all festivals, and said that when applied to Good Friday and Christmas Day it comes close to blasphemy.

BAOR, *n* (abbr) – British Army of the Rhine, the British troops in Germany.

bap, *n* – a soft roll, similar to a hamburger roll.

bargee, *n* – a barge-hand. It can also mean rough clothes such as might be worn by a barge-hand.

barmy, *adj* (col) – crazy. A working-class word.

barney, *n* (col) – a quarrel, row.

baronet, *n* – a title of nobility just below that of baron. A baronet's name is preceded by 'Sir,' but unlike a knighthood, which also rates a 'Sir,' a baronetcy is inherited. A baronet styles himself 'Sir John Smith, bart' to distinguish himself from a knight.

barrack, *v* – to interrupt a speaker with shouts or objections. One of the few words in the British language from the Australian, it was originally an Aborigine word.

barrel organ, *n* – hurdy gurdy.

barrister, *n* – a lawyer who pleads cases in court. The legal profession in Britain is divided into barristers and solicitors (only the former are 'called to the bar') and solicitors mostly do out-of-court work.

barrow, *n* – pushcart.

bash, *v* and *n* – to hit or smash. It also has a number of loose colloquial meanings. To **have a bash** at something means to have a try, to **bash away** means

to struggle on, and it can mean sexual intercourse.

basin, *n* – often, a bowl, as in **pudding basin.**

bath, *v* – to have a bath.

Bath bun, *n* – a small, semi-sweet cake.

Bath chair, *n* – a large wheelchair. Named after the city of Bath, a spa resort popular with invalids since the Roman occupation of Britain.

bath cube, *n* – a cube of bath salts.

bathe, *v* – to go swimming, not to have a bath. See BATH above.

bathroom, *n* – just that. It may not have a toilet; this is often in a separate room by itself. If you want the toilet in Britain it is wise to say so.

baths, *n* – public, municipally-owned baths, usually including a swimming pool and often a meeting hall.

batman, *n* – a senior army or air force officer's personal servant, also a soldier. The word predates Batman and has no connection with him, and is no longer used.

batsman, *n* – the batter in cricket.

batten, *n* – a strip of wood.

beak, *n* (col) – a magistrate, or a schoolteacher.

beano, *n* (col) – a celebration, originally a bean feast.

bearskin, *n* – the tall black fur hat worn by some soldiers on ceremonial guard duty. See also BUSBY.

bed-sitting room, *n* – a room let for a person to live in, or any room that serves as bedroom and living room. Sometimes shortened to **bed-sitter** or **bed-sit**.

Beeb, the, *prop n* – the BBC, the British Broadcasting Corporation.

beefeater, *n* – a Yeoman of the Guard who patrols the Tower of London in a splendid uniform. The office is archaic.

beetle off, *v* (col) – hurry away.

Mrs Beeton, *prop n* – a big book on cookery and household management that was published 100 years ago and was a standby of wives in that century, and is still read today. Known familiarly by the name of the authoress, as Dr Benjamin Spock's book on baby care is known as 'Dr Spock.'

beetroot, *n* – beet.

Belisha beacon, *n* – a pole with an orange ball on top that marks a pedestrian crossing point. Named after Leslie Hore-Belisha, the Minister of Transport who initiated them in 1937.

belt, *v* – to travel at speed.

belt up, *v* – shut up, stop talking.

bend, *n* (col) – **round the bend** means crazy.

bent, *adj* (col) – 1. crooked. A police and underworld term mostly. 2. homosexual or sexually perverted. This use is newish and less common.

berk, *n* (col) – a stupid and disagreeable person. It is a mild term of abuse, though its derivation is obscene: from the rhyming slang phrase 'Berkeley hunt' (see RHYMING SLANG).

bespoke, *adj* – custom-tailored.

bf, *n* (abbr, col) – bloody fool.

big dipper, *n* – roller coaster.

big end, *n* – in a car, the larger end of the connecting rod.

bilberry, *n* – a native fruit similar to a blueberry.

bill, *n* – a restaurant or bar cheek, as well as a bill in a store. The word 'check' is not used for any kind of bill in Britain.

billiards, *n* – a kind of pool.

Billingsgate, *n* – foul, abusive language. Billingsgate is a London fish market where the bad language is proverbial, hence the expression 'the tongue of a fishwife'. It was so 300 years ago, it would seem from a snatch of dialogue from the seventeenth-century play *The Plain Dealer* by William Wycherley:

Quaint: With sharp invectives –

Widow: Alias Billingsgate.

billion, *n* – traditionally, a British billion is 1,000,000 million, a thousand times as much as an American billion. The other multiples are similarly different: a trillion is a million times a billion, and so on. However, the American version of a billion has become widely used in Britain in the last few years.

billycan, *n* – a can for boiling water.

bind, *n* (col) – a drag, an onerous task.

bind over, *v* – to release on conviction, as an alternative to imprisonment, on the promise of good behavior for a specified period, and subject to certain conditions.

bint, *n* (col) – girl. A disrespectful term, an Arabic word brought back by soldiers from the Middle East, where they regarded most girls with disrespect. Working-class.

birch, *v* – to inflict punishment by caning. The stick is usually made of birchwood.

bird, *n* (col) – girl.

biro, *n* – ball-point pen. A trade name that has become a generic term. Pronounced 'by-row'.

biscuit, *n* – cookie, or cracker.

bitter, *n* – the most widely-consumed kind of beer in Britain. (When you order beer in a pub, you always specify the kind: bitter, lager, light ale, or whatever. A Briton would no more ask simply for 'beer' than he would ask in a restaurant for 'meat'.) A time-worn, bi-lingual joke:
     Waiter in a Berlin cocktail lounge: '*Bitte?*'
     British customer: 'No, whisky and soda, please.'

black, *v* – a labor move which involves refusing to work on a product or place, usually in support of other strike action. If unions black a port, members will refuse to move cargoes into or out of it.

black, *n* – to **put up a black** means to commit an egregious error, to blot one's copy-book.

Black and Tans, *prop n* – the British auxiliary police who carried out repressive measures in Ireland during the Anglo-Irish War of 1920–1, so-called because of the color of their uniforms.

blackleg, *n* – a scab in a labor dispute.

blackshirt, *adj* and *n* – fascist.

The British Union of Fascists in the 1930s used to sport black shirts, after the style of Mussolini's followers.

blancmange, *n* – vanilla (or other flavor) pudding. Pronounced 'blamonge'.

blessed, *adj* (col) – an all-purpose adjective, added for emphasis. Working-class. Old-fashioned.

Blighty, *prop n* (col) – Britain, seen from abroad. A First World War word.

blimey, *interj* – a mild exclamation, though it is descended over the centuries from the stronger 'God blind me!' Cockney.

Blimp or **Colonel Blimp,** *n* – an archetypal mossback with old-fashioned, jingoistic attitudes.

blind, *v* (col) – swear, usually used in the phrase **effing and blinding**.

blinkers, *n* – blinders on a horse.

bloater, *n* – a kind of smoked herring.

block or **block of flats,** *n* – apartment house. The word 'block' in the American sense (of a city block) does not exist in Britain, because cities were not laid out in the same way, or, in most cases, laid out at all. 2. a cut, in printing.

bloke, *n* – fellow, guy.

bloody, *adj* (col) – an all-purpose adjective. It rarely has any specific meaning, although in upper-class speech it is occasionally used as a slightly off-color synonym for 'awful', as in 'How perfectly bloody!' It can be attached to any noun for emphasis and, usually, to add a note of exasperation and annoyance, e.g. 'The bloody train's late.' It was once a fairly strong swear word, and when it was first spoken on the stage in Bernard Shaw's *Pygmalion*, audiences 'trembled and shuddered,' as a *New York Times* correspondent reported at the time. But that was in 1912, and there are few places today where its use would cause any quivers. In the more genteel Britain that fought the Second World War, an official British pamphlet for American servicemen advised that 'bloody' was best avoided in mixed company, but was not forbidden to soldiers in battle (there may have been a few GIs who missed the irony). These days, it is often used, incorrectly, as an adverb. e.g. 'He bloody did it!'

bloody-minded, *adj* (col) – in a difficult mood, deliberately unhelpful.

blooming, *adj* (col) – an all-purpose adjective, much as 'bloody' is, but mostly working-class.

blower, *n* – 1. the private telephone lines that link a racetrack with off-course bookmakers. 2. (col) a telephone.

blue, *v* (col) – to spend money impetuously or quickly.

blue, *n* – a letterman at Oxford or Cambridge University in the team which plays against the other.

blue-eyed boy, *n* – fair-haired boy, favorite.

boater, *n* – a flat straw hat.

Boat Race, *prop n* – with the definite article, this always means the annual race between the Oxford and Cambridge University rowing crews. University sports do not attract much interest in Britain and rowing contests even less, but for some reason this has become a major event on everyone's calendar, and is watched with much excitement.

bob, *n* (col) – shilling. The coin that is now, under decimal coinage, 5 pence. 'A bob or two' means a lot of money. 'That bloke's got a bob or two' means he's rich.

bobby, *n* (col) – a policeman. The term derives from the name of the man who, as Home Secretary, created the modern British police forces in 1829, Sir Robert ('Bobby') Peel. Policemen used to be called 'peelers' in the last century, and in Northern Ireland they are still.

boffin, *n* – a scientist or technologist. It came into use during the Second World War as service slang.

bog, *n* (col) – toilet. Army and schoolboy slang.

boiler suit, *n* – overalls.

bollocks, *n* (col) – balls, in the anatomical sense.

bolshie, *adj* (col) – rebellious, refusing to conform or fall into line. An abbreviation of 'Bolshevik'.

bolt hole, *n* (col) – a safe hiding place.

bomb, *n* (col) – 1. a great success, the exact opposite of its meaning in American. 'It was a bomb!' means it was a hit (if a play) or a ball (if a party). It is also used, in a curious grammatical construction, with the verb 'to go'; 'It went a bomb' means it worked out great. The word is newish and used in the modern-minded occupations; it is more likely to be heard among advertising men or movie people than doctors or lawyers, at the Dorchester Bar than the Reform Club. 2. a lot of money, e.g. 'It cost a bomb.'

Bombay duck, *n* – a tropical fish, the bummalo, usually eaten dried with curry.

bonce, *n* (col) – head, brains. Cockney.

bonk, *v* – to hit. A lightweight word, which would not be used about a serious episode.

bonnet, *n* – the hood of a car.

book, *v* – reserve.

Booker prize, *n* – the best-known British literary award, given annually for the best novel.

bookstall, *n* – a newstand.

boot, *n* – 1. the trunk of a car. 2. to **put the boot in** means, literally, to kick someone when he has been knocked down, but is more commonly used metaphorically to mean to press home an advantage to the bitter end.

boot sale, *n* – a sort of collective garage sale. People sell things from the 'boot' – trunk – of their cars.

boozer, *n* (col) – a pub, a drinking place, as often as a person who drinks.

Borstal, *n* – a prison school to which youthful lawbreakers can be sent as an alternative to jail. Now called officially 'youth custody centres'.

bottle, *n* – courage, stamina, strength of character. To **bottle out** is to run away.

bottom drawer, *n* – hope chest.

bottom of the street, *n* – end of the street.

bovver boots, *n* – heavy boots worn by teenage hooligans, useful for kicking.

bowler, *n* – 1. derby hat. 2. in cricket, the man who **bowls** the ball to the batsman.

bowls, *n* – a game played with large balls on a flat lawn, mostly by elderly men, similar to the Italian *bocce*, and quite unlike bowling.

box, *n* (col) – television, the 'boob tube.'

box clever, *v* – to act shrewdly and cunningly.

Boxing Day, *prop n* – 26 December, a public holiday, except in Scotland.

box junction, *n* – a marked-off area at a road junction which you may not enter until there is a clear exit.

braces, *n* – suspenders (suspenders are 'garters').

brambleberry, *n* – another, less common word for 'blackberry'.

brass, *n* – money. North of England term.

brew up, *v* – to make tea.

breathalyser, *n* – a device used by the police to analyze a driver's breath to determine how much alcohol is in his blood. Also a verb, to **breathalyse**.

breve, *n* – a double whole-note. Musical.

bridge roll, *n* – a small, soft sweetish roll in an elongated shape.

brigadier, *n* – equivalent to a brigadier-general.

brief, *n* – a solicitor's instructions to a barrister (see SOLICITOR and BARRISTER) in a court case. By extension, any set of instructions that constitutes an assignment.

brilliantine, *n* – a dressing that adds gloss to the hair.

bristols, *n* (col) – breasts. Cockney.

British Telecom, *prop n* – the national telephone and telecommunications company.

broad bean, *n* – a bean that is the same shape as a lima bean, only greyer and grittier.

broadcloth, *n* – dress or shirting material.

Broadmoor, *prop n* – the institution for the criminally insane.

Broads, *prop n* – see NORFOLK BROADS.

broadsheet, *n* – handbill. Used less than it was.

brolly, *n* (col) – short for 'umbrella'. A woman's word.

brothel-creepers, *n* (col) – men's shoes with thick crepe soles.

brouhaha, *n* – tumult, uproar.

brown ale, *n* – ale that is dark brown in color, a common pub drink.

browned-off, *adj* (col) – fed up.

Brownies, *n* – the junior **Girl Guides** (Girl Scouts).

Brum, *prop n* (abbr, col) – Birmingham (England – the second biggest city – not Alabama). **Brummie** is someone from Birmingham.

BST, *n* (abbr) – British summer time, roughly equivalent to daylight saving time.

Btu, *n* (abbr) – British thermal unit, a measure of heat.

bucket shop, *n* – an office that sells cut-price airline tickets, sometimes in violation of the airlines' pricing rules.

bubble-and-squeak, *n* – potato and cabbage fried together, sometimes with meat.

Buck House, *prop n* (col) – Buckingham Palace. Used mostly by those who are, or like to be thought to be, regular visitors.

budgerigar, *n* – an Australian parakeet, the commonest kind, commonly kept as a pet. Often shortened to **budgie**.

buffer, *n* – 1. the bumper at the end of a railroad track. 2. an old buffer is an elderly stick-in-the mud.

bugger, *v* (col) – as well as its formal meaning, to commit sodomy, this is also a colloquial term that is less nasty than one might suppose from its derivation, and as such has a number of meanings: 1. to foul up, or render useless, e.g. 'That's buggered our plan.' 2. **bugger off** – scram, beat it. 3. in the passive tense, e.g. 'I'm buggered', it means tired-out, exhausted. 4. also in the passive, 'Well, I'll be buggered!' can be a simple expletive like 'Well, I'll be damned!'

bugger, *n* (col) – 1. a person, not necessarily in any pejorative sense. 2. an awful situation. A man in a pub talking about a colleague who had just lost his job said, 'Being out of work with a wife pregnant is a bugger!'

bugger-all, *n* (col) – nothing. See ALL.

building society, *n* – a loan

society that provides mortgages.

bukshee, *adj* (col) – see BAKSHEE.

bull, *n* – rigid and unnecessary military discipline.

bullet, *n* (col) – the sack from a job.

bum, *n* (col) – ass, rectum. This word goes back at least five hundred years, but over the past ten its use among adults has dwindled as the American meaning takes over, though schoolchildren still use it. At least there are not so many puerile jokes now about the confusion of the two meanings.

bum-boy, *n* (col) – homosexual partner. An insulting term.

bumf, *n* (col) – documentation. Though people who use the word blithely don't realize it, it comes from an old army term 'bum-fodder', meaning usable as toilet paper. See BUM.

bummarree, *n* – a porter in a fish market.

bun, *n* – a soft, sweet roll, halfway to being a cake, usually eaten with butter. Colloquially, to have **a bun in the oven** means to be pregnant.

bun-fight, *n* (col) – a humorous term for a tea party or other social occasion.

bung, *v* (col) – throw, toss.

bunk off, *v* (col) – to skip classes in school. Newish.

BUPA, *n* – acronym for the largest private health insurance scheme, the British United Provident Association.

bureau, *n* – a large, heavy desk with pigeon holes.

Burke's Peerage, *prop n* – the standard bloodstock and heraldic guide to the nobility and baronets, which traces their lineage. See DEBRETT'S.

Burton, *prop n* – a kind of beer, named for the town where it is brewed. In RAF slang, to **go for a Burton** means to be killed. Sometimes it is used to mean a thing is broken, as in 'My watch has gone for a Burton'.

busby, *n* – a tall fur hat with a bag hanging from the top, worn by Hussars in the British Army. It is used commonly to describe the tall black fur hats worn by the soldiers on ceremonial guard duty outside the royal palaces, but the army will not accept this term for them, and calls these 'bearskins'.

bushel, *n* – 2,219 cubic inches, against an American bushel's 2,150 cubic inches.

busker, *n* – street musician.

butchers, *n* (col) – a look at something, as in 'Let's have a butchers at it'. Rhyming slang (butcher's hook).

butter bean, *n* – lima bean.

butter-up, *v* (col) – to sweet-talk, flatter.

butty, *n* (col) – sandwich. Mostly Northern and working-class.

buzz-off, *v* (col) – scram.

by-law, *n* – municipal ordinance.

by-word, *n* – household word, often standing for something as in 'His name was a by-word for dishonesty.'

C

cack-handed, *adj* (col) – clumsy.

cadge, *v* – to borrow, or beg.

café, *n* – a cheap restaurant or snack bar. Often pronounced 'caff'.

cake-hole, *n* – mouth.

call box, *n* – telephone booth.

call-up, *n* – the draft.

camp bed, *n* – cot. A cot in Britain is a bed for a small child.

can, *n* (col) – to **carry the can** means to be shouldered with the blame for something that is someone else's fault.

Cantabrian, *n* and *adj* – a graduate of Cambridge University, or, as an adjective, referring to Cambridge.

canvasser, *n* – someone who solicits votes for a candidate, or takes a poll on behalf of one.

caravan, *n* – trailer.

card punch, *n* – key punch.

cards, *n* (col) – in common parlance, one's cards are one's National Insurance papers, held by an employer, who has to put a stamp on them weekly signifying payment of his contribution. When a working man is **given his cards,** he is fired.

caretaker, *n* – janitor.

Carey Street, *prop n* (col) – the location of the bankruptcy court in London; hence, to be in Carey Street is to be bankrupt. (One is in a street in Britain, not on it. Only a streetwalker is 'on the streets'.)

car park, *n* – parking lot.

carriage, *n* – railroad or subway car.

carrier bag, *n* – shopping bag.

carve-up, *n* – a swindle perpetrated by a number of people.

cashier, *n* – teller.

castor sugar, *n* – very fine granulated sugar.

casual, *adj* – **casual work** is irregular paid work, usually by the day. A **casual worker** is someone who works on this basis rather than for a regular wage.

catapult, *n* – slingshot.

cat's eyes, *n* – reflectors on a road surface to guide drivers at night.

cat's pyjamas or **cat's whiskers,** *n* (col) – the greatest ever, as in 'He thinks he's the cat's pyjamas'. It is dated, contemporary with 'the bees' knees'.

caucus, *n* – a permanent group within a political party. This word changed meaning slightly when it crossed over from America.

CBE, *n* (abbr) – Commander of the Order of the British Empire, a title awarded for services to the community.

cellarman, *n* – a man who works behind the scenes in a pub.

centenary, *n* – centennial. Pronounced 'centeenery'.

central reservation, *n* – divider on a road.

chairman, *n* – the senior executive of a business.

chambers, *n* – a barrister's (see) office.

champers, *n* (col) – champagne. This is an upper-class usage, in which the suffix 'er' is added to the first syllable of a word. Eric Partridge, in his *Dictionary of Slang and Unconventional English* says it began at Oxford in 1875 and came out of there with the bright young things in the 1920s. Occasionally, this is applied to ordinary words, e.g. **preggers** – pregnant, but more often to a name, to denote easy familiarity. Thus, the Wig and Pen Club is known to the lawyers and journalists who comprise its membership as **the Wiggers,** and among Britons all over the Far East, the local branch of the Hong Kong and Shanghai Bank is **the Honkers and Shankers.**

Chancellor of the Duchy of Lancaster, *prop n* – an archaic post often given to someone of real political importance to give him a seat in the cabinet.

Chancellor of the Exchequer, *prop n* – the equivalent to the Secretary of the Treasury.

Channel, *prop n* – the English Channel.

chapel, *n* – 1. any nonconformist (see NONCONFORMIST)

church. Also, as in America, a small place of worship for any Christian denomination. 2. a local in any of the unions in the print or newspaper industries.

char, *v* – to do menial housework for someone else. The word is a corruption of 'chore'.

char, *n* – 1. a person paid to do the housework. Also **charlady.** 2. (col) tea. Working-class.

charabanc, *n* – a long-distance sightseeing bus. Sometimes shortened to **chara.** An old-fashioned word for it.

charge hand, *n* – the head of a crew of workmen.

charge sheet, *n* – the police record of arrests.

charlie, *n* – fool.

charlies, *n* (col) – breasts.

cheesed-off, *adj* – fed up, annoyed.

cheese-paring, *adj* – penny-pinching.

chemist, *n* – druggist. A chemist's shop is a drugstore, but it sells a much more limited range of goods than an American drugstore, and has no soda fountain.

Chequers, *prop n* – the Prime Minister's official country residence.

chesterfield, *n* – a heavily-padded sofa.

chicory, *n* – endive.

chief executive, *n* – recently, this has come to mean sometimes the working head of a business.

chimney, *n* – smokestack. (But on a ship a smokestack is a **funnel.**)

Chindits, *prop n* – an élite and much-admired force that fought behind the Japanese lines in Burma in the Second World War.

chipolata, *n* – a skinny sausage.

chippings, *n* – bits of stone which can flake off a cliff. An American tourist driving through England was puzzled because after passing through the village of Chipping Sodbury, he passed three signs saying 'Loose chippings', but he never came to it.

chippy, *n* (col) – fish-and-chip shop.

chips, *n* – French fried potatoes.

chit, *n* (col) – pass, document or other piece of paper. Originally a service slang word, and like many others, stemming from a Hindi word that the army brought back from India.

chivvy, *v* – to prod, press someone for action.

choked, *adj* (col) – angry, resentful. Working-class.

choker, *n* – 1. neckerchief or scarf. A working-class term, though it was once high fashion. 2. a necklace fitting tightly around the neck.

chop, *n* (col) – to **get the chop** means to be fired, or to be killed, depending on the context.

chopper, *n* – cleaver.

Christmas box, *n* – a Christmas present, usually one given to someone who provides service, such as a janitor or milkman. See BOXING DAY.

Christmas pudding, *n* – plum pudding.

chuck, *v* – to throw. **chuck it,** *v* (col) – to stop, desist, call it off.

chuck or **chuck steak,** *n* – stewing meat.

chucker-out, *n* – bouncer.

chuffed, *adj* (col) – pleased.

church warden, *n* – a lay official of a Church of England parish.

churn, *n* – a large milk can as well as a butter-making machine.

CID, *n* (abbr) – Criminal Investigation Department, the plain-clothes branch of a police force.

cider, *n* – a drink made from fermented apples, but in Britain this is always alcoholic.

circular saw, *n* – buzz saw.

City, *prop n* – the old City of London, or the financial world of which it is the center. 'Opinion in the City' means the same thing that 'opinion on Wall Street' would mean in America. 'He's something in the City' means he is a financial executive.

City editor, *n* – the financial editor of a newspaper.

Civil List, *prop n* – the system by which Parliament provides money for the royal household.

civvy street, *n* (col) – civilian life. A service term.

cladding, *n* – a covering of any kind on a structure, e.g. 'wood cladding on bathroom walls'.

clanger, *n* – a conspicuous mistake, a resounding gaffe.

clapped-out, *adj* (col) – worn out, exhausted.

claret, *n* – blood. The term is much used in underworld and boxing circles.

clawback, *n* – a retrieval of money paid, for instance, through tax relief paid back at the end of the year.

clever dick, *n* – smart alec.

clippie, *n* – a woman bus conductor who issues tickets.

cloakroom, *n* – often a euphemism for toilet.

clobber, *n* – kit, equipment, or else clothes, usually for the job. 'His common clobber and Noddy car seemed to be making another kind of statement.' From an article in the *Guardian* (July 16 1983) about best-selling author Jack Higgins. See COMMON and NODDY.

close, *adj* – as a description of the weather, it means heavy, humid, stifling.

clot, *n* (col) – a fool. The word is of the 1940s, and today has a period flavour about it.

cloth cap, *n* – pertaining to the traditional lifestyle of the working class.

clotted cream, *n* – very thick cream, a country specialty of Devon and Cornwall.

clueless, *adj* (col) – ignorant, 'without a clue'.

coach, *n* – long-distance bus.

cobblers, *n* (col) – balls in the anatomical sense. Often used metaphorically, e.g. 'His story is a load of old cobblers.'

cock, *n* (col) – 1. nonsense, as in 'that's a lot of cock'. Norman Schurr, in his book *British Self-Taught*, points out that the expression 'cock and bull story' has been divided up, the cock becoming British and the bull American. 2. a familiar form of address to a man, as in 'Hello, old cock'.

cockle, *n* – a tiny edible shellfish, sold by the half-pint from pushcarts, an old-fashioned trade that is dying out slowly. ('Cockles and mussels, alive, alive-o', as the old street cry and the song has it.)

Cockney, *prop n* and *adj* – a working-class accent and argot found mostly in East London, or the person who uses it. In the rest of Britain, a Cockney is any working-class Londoner. By tradition, a Cockney is someone born within the sound of Bow Bells (the bells of St Mary-le-Bow Church).

cock-up, *n* (col) – a mess, a fouled-up situation. Rather vulgar.

cod, *n* and *adj* – joke, spoof or parody. A sophisticated word.

codswallop, *n* (col) – nonsense, rubbish. This has an interesting derivation, though most Britons are unaware of it. One Hiram Codd patented a particular shape of bottle in the 1870s that contained lemonade. **Wallop** is a slang word for bitter beer; hence, beer-drinkers came to call very weak beer 'Codd's wallop', and later the term came to be applied to anything with no substance.

college, *n* – 1. an institute of higher education that does not have the status of a university or award a degree. 2. a school within the university at Oxford, Cambridge or London Universities. 3. some public (private) schools that style themselves colleges.

Colonel Blimp, *n* – see BLIMP.

combinations, *n* – union suit.

come-uppance, *n* – just desserts, as in 'He got his come-uppance'.

comforter, *n* – a woollen scarf.

commercial traveller, *n* – traveling salesman. Often shortened to **traveller** (note spelling).

commis chef, *n* – a lowly assistant in a restaurant kitchen. The first word is pronounced 'commey'.

commissionaire, *n* – uniformed doorman.

commis waiter, *n* – bus boy.

common, *n* – a piece of public parkland.

common, *adj* – lower-class. The word reeks of uptight, lower-middle-class snobbery, and is given its place by Noël Coward in some sentiments he puts into a woman's mouth in his play *Fumed Oak*: 'She's common for one thing, she dyes her hair for another, and she's a bit too free and easy all round for my taste.'

commoner, *n* – anyone who is not of noble rank.

common-or-garden, *adj* – ordinary, standard model. The term comes from gardening catalogues.

Commons, *n* – short for 'House of Commons'.

compère, *n* – master of ceremonies.

compositor, *n* – typesetter.

comprehensive school, *n* – a public high school that includes both the more and less educationally advanced pupils, unlike those which take one or the other.

concert party, *n* – a vaudeville show put on at some place other than a regular theater, i.e. a park, seafront promenade, summer camp.

conk, *n* (col) – nose.

conker, *n* – the hard brown nut in a horse chestnut. British

schoolboys collect these, and play a game with them called **conkers**.

Conservative, *n* – a member of the Conservative Party, one of the two major political parties. This does not imply being as far to the right as it would in America.

Consols, *n* – the financial world's term for the British Government's consolidated annuities.

constable, *n* – an ordinary policeman. See also PC. A police chief is a **chief constable**.

constituency, *n* – district in the political sense; a parliamentary constituency is the equivalent of a congressional district.

consultant, *n* – the senior rank of doctor in a hospital.

convenience, *n* – public toilet.

conversion, *n* – a house converted into separate apartments.

conveyancing, *n* – the legal arrangements for the transfer of a piece of property.

cop, *v* (col) – to get something unpleasant, e.g. 'He copped a five-pound fine'. In service slang, to **cop it** sometimes means to be killed.

copper-bottomed, *adj* (col) – sound, thorough. I've heard talk of 'copper-bottomed shares' and 'a copper-bottomed bastard'.

cop shop, *n* (col) – police station.

copy taster, *n* – a person on a newspaper who looks at incoming copy and decides what should be done with it.

cordial, *n* – 1. a sweet liqueur. 2. a concentrated, non-alcoholic fruit flavoring, to be mixed with water to make up a soft drink.

cords, *n* (col) – corduroy pants.

corn, *n* – all edible grains.

corn dolly, *n* – a decoration made of corn stalks, sometimes in the shape of a dolly, a popular souvenir in country areas.

corned beef, *n* – processed meat. American-style corned beef is called **salt beef.**

cornet, *n* – cone, as in 'ice cream cone'.

cornflour, *n* – cornstarch.

corporation, *n* – municipal government. People who work for the municipality may be called **corporation employees.**

cosh, *n* – a club, or stick shaped into a weapon. Also a verb, **to cosh** – to hit with a club.

cos lettuce, *n* – romaine lettuce.

coster or **costermonger,** *n* – someone who sells things from a pushcart.

cot, *n* – a crib for a very small child, usually a small bed with sides. A **crib** in Britain is for a new-born baby only. A **cot** (American) is a **camp bed. cot death,** *n* – the sudden, unexplained death of an infant while asleep, SIDS, sudden infant death syndrome.

cotton, *n* – thread.

cotton wool, *n* – absorbent cotton.

council flat or **council house,** *n* – an apartment of house rented or bought from the local authority, often at a subsidized price. Characteristically working-class housing.

counsel, *n* – a barrister retained by a solicitor to plead a case in court (see **BARRISTER**).

county family, *n* – an old-established, upper-class country family. As an adjective, **county** refers to the lifestyle.

county school, *n* – a public school (in the American rather than the British sense) coming under a local council, usually in a rural area.

coursing, *n* – the so-called sport of hunting hares with dogs.

courtesy title, *n* – title given by custom and not legal right, such as the titles commonly given to members of a noble family other than the head. For instance, the eldest son of a duke commonly takes the title 'Marquess of ——' (his father's second title), and all the children of a viscount are styled 'The Honourable'.

Coventry, *prop n* – if someone is **sent to Coventry** it means that the people who send him refuse to talk to him.

cracking, *v* (col) – to **get cracking** means to get moving to take vigorous action, get on with the job.

Cranwell, *prop n* – the Royal Air Force academy.

crash barrier, *n* – a central rail or other barrier separating the traffic on an express highway.

crayfish, *n* – crawfish.

crib, *n* – 1. a crib, but one for a new-born baby only. After that, the infant sleeps in a slightly larger bed which is called a **cot.** 2. in school or college, a pony, something from which answers to an exam can be copied.

crib, *v* – to copy, usually illicitly.

crispbread, *n* – any one of the crackers that are bread substitutes.

crisps, *n* – potato chips.

crock, *n* – an old car or, facetiously, an aged and infirm person, e.g. 'I've got a backache today; I'll be a real old crock soon.'

crocodile, *n* – a line of schoolchildren walking along.

croft, *n* – a small farm in Scotland. A **crofter** farms one.

crotchet, *n* – quarter-note. Musical.

cruet, *n* – a set of containers for condiments at the table, usually salt, pepper and mustard. It does not mean a bottle, as in America.

crumpet, *n* – 1. a flat yeast cake for toasting. 2. (col) sex, or a girl available as a sexual partner. There are many old vaudeville sketches around this double entendre, typically with a white-moustached colonel sitting on a colonial verandah saying that now he's had his tea he feels like some crumpet.

crush barrier, *n* – barrier erected to contain crowds.

CSE, *n* (abbr) – certificate of secondary education, usually awarded at age about sixteen, ranking slightly lower academically than GCE or O-levels (see O–LEVELS).

CS gas, *n* – the riot gas used by British security forces, similar to mace in its effects.

cup, *n* – as a measure in cooking, 10 ounces, slightly more than in America.

cupboard, *n* – closet; 'closet' dropped out of use in Britain a couple of centuries ago; a remnant is WC (for 'water closet') meaning toilet.

cup final, *n* – the biggest soccer match of the season, for the national championship.

cuppa, *n* (col) – cup of tea.

curate, *n* – an assistant vicar.

curate's egg, *n* – something that is good in parts and bad in parts. The allusion is to a cartoon in *Punch* in 1895. A curate is staying with his ecclesiastical superior. The host apologizes at breakfast because his guest's egg is stale, and the curate, desperately anxious to please, says, 'Oh no, I assure you, parts of it are excellent.'

currant loaf, *n* – loaf of raisin bread.

current account, *n* – checking account at a bank.

curriculum vitae, *n* – a resumé of one's career, such as is sent with a job application. Often abbreviated to cv.

cushy, *adj* (col) – easy, soft. Originally a wartime service term.

cutting, *n* – clipping, in the Press or horticultural sense, e.g. a clipping from a newspaper or from a bush.

cut-throat, *n* (col) – an open-bladed, or straight razor.

cut-up, *adj* (col) – upset, as in 'He's very cut-up about it'. Upper-class, and with a stiff upper-lip tone.

D

Dame, *n* – a title conferred on a woman equivalent to a knighthood. There is also a pantomime dame, who is a comic character in a Christmas entertainment. See PANTOMIME.

damn-all, *n* (col) – absolutely nothing. See ALL.

damp course, *n* – an insulating layer to protect a building against rising damp.

Darby and Joan, *prop n* – the archetypal elderly happily-married couple. There are Darby and Joan clubs in many localities.

Dartmouth, *prop n* – the Royal Naval College, equivalent of Annapolis.

davenport, *n* – an antique folding writing-desk.

dead, *adj* (col) – very. Cockney.

death duties, *n* – estate tax. Strictly speaking the term is obsolete, although it is widely used, because the tax is subsumed in others.

de-bag, *v* – to take the pants off someone as a joke.

Debrett's Peerage, *prop n* – a Who's Who of British peers. It is accurate as far as possible, and technically, at least, undeserving of Oscar Wilde's often-quoted crack, put into the mouth of one of the characters in his play *A Woman of No*

Importance: 'You should study the peerage, Gerald. . . . It's the best thing in fiction that the English have ever done.'

decorator, *n* – a house-painter and paper-hanger.

decree nisi, *n* – a divorce decree that becomes effective ('absolute' in British legal parlance) only after a stated period, usually three months. This allows time for the court to rescind it if it seems that the terms, such as financial ones, are not being complied with.

deed poll, *n* – a legal declaration of intention, most commonly used in changing one's name.

dekko, *n* (col) – a look, a glimpse. Another word brought back from the Orient.

demerara, *n* – a brown, crystallized sugar from the West Indies.

demo, *n* (col) – a common abbreviaion of 'demonstration', in the political sense.

demob, *n* and *v* (col) – discharge from the services. From 'demobilize'.

deposit account, *n* – savings account at a bank.

dessert spoon, *n* – as a measure in cooking, it is 2 teaspoons.

detached, *adj* – of a house, separated from the buildings on either side. **semi-detached**

means separated on one side and joined on the other; in Britain, houses are often built in tandem. **semi** is a common term for a semi-detached house.

diabolical, *adj* (col) – bad, awful in the sense of incompetent rather than nasty; someone's acting or cooking might be described as 'diabolical'.

dicey, *adj* – risky, uncertain.

dicky, *adj* – not working properly.

dicky bird, *n* – word, used only in the negative, e.g. 'not a dicky bird'. Rhyming slang.

dicky seat, *n* – rumble seat, if anyone remembers what that is.

diddle, *v* (col) – gyp.

digestive biscuit, *n* – a soft, wholemeal cookie.

digs, *n* – furnished lodgings. Also, occasionally, **diggings**.

dim, *adj* – stupid, thick-headed. An American would say 'dim-witted'.

dinner jacket, *n* – tuxedo.

direct grant school, *n* – private school that receives a subsidy from the government with the proviso that it takes many pupils without fees.

directly, *adv* – immediately. Used much less than it was.

director, *n* – a member of the governing board of a business corporation (or **limited company**, in British terminology). A director of a company may take no part in the day-to-day running of it. One who does is often called an **executive director**.

directory inquiries, *n* – (on the telephone) information. If you want to know a number, you ask for this.

dispensary, *n* – the department of a chemist's (drugstore) or hospital that makes up and dispenses medicines.

district commissioner, *n* – a government official in a colonial territory with powers to enforce law and adjudicate disputes. With the fading of empire, the office has become obsolete.

divider, *n* – central reservation on a road dividing two directions of traffic.

DIY, *n* (abbr) – do-it-yourself. Department stores have DIY departments for the home handyman.

do, *v* (col) – 1. to get, in an aggressive sense, as in 'I'll do you.' In this sense it is often used jokingly. 2. to cheat. Used mostly, though not exclusively, in the passive mood, as in 'I've been done.'

do, *n* (col) – a party or other social function. More broadly, it can sometimes mean any arranged event involving a number of people; I have heard a bloody commando raid described as a 'dicey do.'

dock, *v* – to withhold part of a salary or regular payment.

dock, *n* – the enclosed area in a courtroom where the prisoner sits.

doctor, *v* – to neuter an animal.

doddle, *n* (col) – a pushover, something easy. Cockney.

dodge, *n* – a shrewd and artful expedient.

dodgem car, *n* – bumper car.

dodgy, *adj* (col) – risky, or questionable in some way, often legally.

do for, *v* – to clean up and keep house for someone. If a bachelor has someone coming in a few times a week to clean up and cook, she will say, 'I do for him.'

dogsbody, *n* (col) – someone who does the odd jobs that no one else wants to do.

do in, *v* (col) – to kill, or, if about a machine rather than a person, to wreck.

doings, *n* (col) – thingamajig.

dollar, *n* (col) – 25 pence. This dates back to before World War II when a dollar was worth 5 shillings. Dated.

dollop, *n* (col) – a large serving.

dolly-bird or **dolly-girl,** *n* – a young and pretty girl, by implication long on sex appeal and short on brains.

don, *n* – a member of the teaching staff at one of the older universities.

donkey's years, *n* (col) – a long time.

doodah, *n* – thingamajik.

doolally, *adj* (col) – weak in the head.

dormitory, *n* – a room in which a lot of people sleep, as in a boarding school. It does *not* mean a building, as in American. An American college teacher was talking to a British counterpart in England recently and remarked that at his college, male and female undergraduates now sleep in the same dormitory. 'Ye Gods!' said the Englishman, and they talked at cross purposes for some time.

doss, *v* – to sleep rough.

doss house, *n* – flop-house.

dotty, *adj* – crazy or zany. A genteel term, usually used flippantly.

double cream, *n* – whipping cream.

doughnut, *n* – a round, sweet pastry, with sugar on the outside and jam or cream inside. It is quite different from an American doughnut.

Downing Street, *prop n* – the small street in London containing the official residences of the Prime Minister (No. 10) and Chancellor of the Exchequer (No. 11).

downs, *n* – undulating tracks of pasture land.

DPP, *prop n* (abbr) – the Director of Public Prosecutions, the government official who is the final arbiter on whether or not someone is prosecuted for an alleged offence.

dram, *n* – a drink of whisky. It was originally a measure.

draper, *n* – a person who sells cloth and certain clothes. The word is somewhat archaic, but is still occasionally used at the top end of the trade.

draughts, *n* – checkers.

drawing pin, *n* – thumb tack.

dress down, *v* – tell off, formally.

dresser, *n* – a kitchen sideboard.

dressing gown, *n* – bathrobe.

dropsy, *n* (col) – a bribe, meaning something dropped in the pocket.

dry, *adj* – a political term that came in during Margaret Thatcher's premiership: it means a hard-line supporter of tough Conservative economic policies. It arose because those members of Thatcher's Conservative Party who were lukewarm in their support came to be called 'wets'.

dual carriageway, *n* – divided highway.

duck, *n* – a score of zero in cricket, sometimes used in other situations.

ducks, *n* – 1. white flannels. 2. (col) a term of endearment.

dumb, *n* – mute, bereft of speech. It does not usually mean stupid. The English writer Edward Shanks once wrote in an article about his travels in America of his bewilderment at hearing someone say: 'My sister Annabelle is dumb; she never stops talking.'

dummy, *n* – baby's pacifier.

Durex, *prop n* – the most common kind of male contraceptive.

dustbin, *n* – garbage pail.

dust cover or **dust jacket,** *n* – book cover.

duster, *n* – dust cloth.

dustman, *n* – garbage collector.

dust-up, *n* (col) – fight row.

Dutch courage, *n* – courage inspired by alcohol. Walter Scott has the hero of *Redgauntlet*, facing a daunting romantic entanglement, push aside liquor with the words: 'Not a drop. No Dutch courage for me.'

duvet, *n* – a large quilt that serves as a substitute for blankets on a bed. Pronounced 'doovay'.

E

each-way, *adj* – a bet on a horse to win, place or show.

early closing, *n* – the day of the week in each district when the stores close in the afternoon, to give the people who work in them a half-day off. 'Savannah has all the pace of an English village during early closing.' – Richard Neville in the London *Evening Standard*, July 20, 1972.

earnest, *n* – a promise, or at least an indication, of what is to follow. Used often in legal correspondence, e.g. 'We are sending you a deposit as an earnest of our intention to proceed with this matter.'

earth wire, *n* – ground wire.

East Anglia, *prop n* – the area of eastern England that bulges out into the North Sea.

East End, *prop n* – the part of London containing most of the older poorer neighborhoods. See also WEST END.

eccles cake, *n* – a flat cake with a filling of dried fruit and spice.

egg flip, *n* – eggnog.

eiderdown, *n* – quilt.

elastic band, *n* – rubber band.

eleven-plus, *n* – an exam taken at the age of eleven to decide which of two streams of secondary education a child will enter. Abolished recently; the two streams are now merged in most places, but the issue is controversial and the exam could be brought back.

elevenses, *n* – a mid-morning snack.

engaged, *adj* – busy, of a telephone line. 'The number is engaged', means that the line is busy.

enjoin, *v* – to compel by law, or else to urge strongly. The opposite of the American meaning.

erk, *n* (col) – the lowest rank in the air force or navy.

Esquire, *n* – a form of written address, added after the name of someone who does not have any title or rank in formal or polite correspondence. Mr John Smith is 'John Smith, Esq.' (the word is not written in full). However, Lord Smith or Major John Smith would not have an 'Esq.' Originally, the term denoted status, and only a member of the property-owning class rated it. But in the age of the common man, hierarchical distinctions are reduced, and everyone gets something before or after his name, as at a children's party where there are competitive games but everybody gets some kind of prize.

estate car, *n* – station wagon.

excuse-me dance, *n* – a dance in which anyone may cut in. A little staid and old-fashioned in the discotheque age.

ex-directory, *adj* – unlisted, of a telephone number.

express, *n* – special delivery: a postal term.

ex-serviceman, *n* – veteran. The word 'veteran' in British implies old age. A **vet** is a veterinary surgeon.

ex-works, *adj* – direct from the factory. A term often used in commerce.

F

fag, *n* – 1. (col) a cigarette. 2. (col) a dreary or onerous task. 3. traditionally, at some public schools (in the British sense) this was a boy assigned to a senior boy as his part-time servant, though the practice has now been dropped. See FAG in the American/British section.

fagged-out, *adj* (col) – tired-out.

faggot, *n* – a fried ball of chopped meat and oatmeal. A North of England specialty.

fancy, *v* – like, or want, as in 'Do you fancy her?' and 'He fancies himself,' both common expressions.

fancy goods, *n* – small decorative objects: the term is used mostly by stores.

fanny, *n* – vagina. Vulgar. Actually, the word is almost archaic, and rarely used these days, but is included here as a warning against using the American word. It came into use in the eighteenth century, after John Cleland's bawdy novel *Fanny Hill – Memoirs of a Woman of Pleasure*.

Fanny Adams or (sometimes) **sweet Fanny Adams**, *n* (col) – nothing, or something that's useless. Sometimes abbreviated to **sweet f.a.** It has a complex and macabre derivation. Fanny Adams was an unfortunate woman whose husband, in 1867, murdered her and chopped her body into small pieces, a crime reported widely and in detail. At about this time the Royal Navy issued canned chopped meat to its crew for the first time, and the sailors, with lurid inventiveness, immediately dubbed this 'Fanny Adams.' The term stayed in the navy for a long time, where it came to mean any food not worth eating, and then, anything worthless.

farthing, *n* – the smallest denomination of money (a quarter of an old penny) until it was withdrawn from circulation in 1960; the word is still used by old-timers to denote a trivial amount of money, e.g. UPI reporting its demise: 'Britain today withdrew the farthing from circulation as a coin of the realm because, after 800 years, it isn't worth a farthing any more.'

Father Christmas, *prop n* – Santa Claus. Both terms are used.

fen or **fenland**, *n* – low-lying marshy land. **The Fens** are a low-lying part of Cambridgeshire.

fête, *n* – a village fair.

fiddle, *v* and *n* (col) – cheat,

gyp. A lightweight word that does not usually carry a tone of serious condemnation. As a verb, it takes an impersonal predicate, i.e. 'he fiddled his expenses', not 'he fiddled the boss'.

filter sign, *n* – a traffic light beckoning on one stream of traffic to turn a corner while the other remains stationary.

fire, *n* – a gas or electric heater.

fire brigade, *n* – fire department.

firefly, *n* – lightning bug.

first, *n* – at university a degree with first-class honors.

first floor, *n* – second floor. The British start counting floors one above the ground, which is always called the ground floor, so that what Americans call the second floor Britons call the first, and so on.

First Sea Lord, *prop n* – commander of the navy, equivalent to the US Chief of Naval Operations.

fishmonger's, *n* – fish store.

fish slice, *n* – a spatula, in the kitchen.

fitted carpet, *n* – wall-to-wall carpeting.

fives, *n* – a kind of handball played at some schools. It requires a special court.

fixture, *n* – a scheduled sporting event.

fixtures and fittings or **f. and f.,** *n* – the non-movable furnishings in an apartment, such as lights and built-in furniture, plus things not easily transferable, such as drapes and carpets. These are often sold with the transfer of an apartment.

flake out, *v* – to collapse with exhaustion.

flakers, *adj* (col) – tired out (see under CHAMPERS for the significance of the 'ers' ending). Upper-class. Another form is **Harry Flakers**.

flaming, *adj* (col) – an adjective added to a word for emphasis, usually indicating annoyance, like 'bloody'.

flan, *n* – an open pie. **flan-case,** *n* – the pastry part of a flan, with the filling to be added.

flannel – 1. as a noun, washcloth. 2. as noun and verb (col), half-truths or untruths designed to cover up something, soft soap. As a verb it means to dish out soft soap.

flasher, *n* (col) – an exhibitionist, in the sexual sense.

flat, *n* – apartment.

flat-out, *adj* – all-out.

flautist, *n* – flutist.

Fleet Street, *prop n* – the center of London's newspaper district, hence, national newspaper journalism. 'He's landed a job in Fleet Street', does not describe the location of his office but the nature of the job.

flex, *n* – electric wire.

flibbertigibbet, *n* – a flighty, mercurial girl; though historically it means an imp or impish person, and could be applied to a male.

flick-knife, *n* – switchblade knife.

flimsy, *n* – a sheet of thin typing paper, or a copy of something on one.

flipping, *adj* (col) – an all-purpose adjective added for emphasis, mostly working-class. Clearly a euphemism.

fluid ounce, *n* – 1.73 cubic inches, against 1.80 cubic inches in an American fluid ounce.

flutter, *n* (col) – a small bet.

fly, *adj* – shrewd, wily, knowing the angles, perhaps dishonest.

flyover, *n* – overpass.

football, *n* – soccer.

forces, *n* – the armed services.

form, *n* – 1. a class or grade at school, the *n*th form rather than the *n*th grade. 2. in racing, a horse's track record. 3. as a colloquial extension of 2., in underworld language it means criminal record.

founder member, *n* – charter member.

Fred Karno's Army, *n* (col) – any military unit of comic ineffectiveness; after a famous vaudeville act of the 1900s. It was first used by British soldiers in the First World War, about themselves, mockingly. Troops who were to fight heroically marched off singing a song that began:

> We are Fred Karno's Army,
> The ragtime infantry.
> We cannot shoot, we cannot fight,
> What bloody use are we . . .

Free Churches, *prop n* – nonconformist churches, Protestant churches other than the Church of England.

freehold, *adj* – used about property, it means without any legal encumbrances. 'For sale freehold' means available for outright purchase, as distinct from leasehold.

french polish, *n* – a high gloss polish used on furniture.

fridge, *n* – a common term for a refrigerator.

fringe, *n* – bangs.

FRS, *n* (abbr) – Fellow of the Royal Society, one of the highest honors that can be conferred on a British scientist.

front bench, *n* – the two central, facing benches in the House of Commons, one occupied by the leaders of the Government, the other by those of the Opposition; see BACK BENCHES.

fruit, old, *n* – rather archaic expression, equivalent of 'old boy.'

fruit cup, *n* – a drink made of fruits, often with wine.

fruit machine, *n* – one-armed bandit.

FT index, *prop n* – the index of representative shares prepared each day by the *Financial Times* newspaper, taken as a guide to the state of the stock market, by TV and radio news, for instance.

fug, *n* – a smoky, stuffy atmosphere. Pronounced carefully.

full stop, *n* – period.

funk, *n* – fright. 'In a blue funk' means terrified. A **funk hole** is a hideout in time of danger.

funnel, *n* – smokestack.

G

gaffer, *n* (col) – boss. Working-class.

gallon, *n* – 277.42 cubic inches, about one-sixth more than a US gallon.

game, *n* (col) – prostitution, used today only in the phrase **on the game**, meaning working as a prostitute. The term has a long lineage, viz, a letter written in the early 1700s by the dramatist Colley Cibber to Alexander Pope: '. . . a certain house of carnal recreation near the Haymarket, where his Lordship's frolic was . . . a girl of the game.'

gammon, *n* – thick cuts of ham, usually served with vegetables as a meat course, or the meatiest cuts of bacon.

gammy, *adj* (col) – unfit or injured, of a limb, e.g. 'He's got a gammy leg.'

ganger, *n* – the foreman of gang of workmen; a straw boss.

garden, *n* – any plot of ground that's cultivated, or adjoins a house. Most Americans' yards would be gardens in England. Britons call it a yard only if it is paved with concrete.

gas, *v* (col) – to talk emptily. Rather upper-class.

gash, *n* – spare parts, or, more often, left-over bits and pieces which can serve as spares.

gasometer, *n* – a gas storage tank.

gateau, *n* – a rich creamy cake. A Gallicism often used, particularly by people selling them.

gazump, *v* – to raise the price of property after someone has agreed to buy it. The term has only recently come into use. It comes from an archaic colloquial term 'gazumph', to swindle, which in turn comes from the Yiddish.

GBH, *n* (abbr) – grievous bodily harm. Police and legal jargon for inflicting this.

GCE, *n* (abbr) – General Certificate of Education, one of a series of certificates for passing exam stages, usually at ages 15–17.

gear, *n* (col) – clothes. A newish, youthful term.

gearbox, *n* – transmission.

gearing, *n* – what Wall Street calls leverage; the ratio in a company between capital and money that is borrowed. A financial term.

gear lever, *n* – gear shift.

geezer, *n* (col) – a bloke, a guy, usually odd in some way.

gelignite, *n* – an explosive made from nitroglycerine, nitrocotton, potassium acid and wood pulp, much used in mining, for safe-blowing and by the IRA.

gen, *n* and *v* (col) – information. It comes from the services, where it was an abbreviation of 'intelligence'. It is also used as a verb: 'I'll gen you up on the situation', means 'I'll fill you in'. **Genned up** means well-informed. A baroque use of the word that's heard occasionally is to **de-gen**, meaning to extract information from someone.

general factotum, *n* – someone who does general duties.

gentrification, *n* (col) – the process of raising the social class level of a street or district.

gentry, *n* – ladies and gentlemen of good breeding. In bygone days, it meant specifically the class of landowners ranking just below the nobility.

Geordie, *n* (col) – someone from Tyneside, the river Tyne area in northeast England with Newcastle at its center.

George Cross, *prop n* – a medal awarded for civilian bravery.

geyser, *n* – a gas-operated device for heating water. It also refers to the natural phenomenon.

ghoulies, *n* (col) – testicles. Upper-class, boarding school and service slang.

giggle, *n* (col) – a lark, something done just for fun. A Cockney term, but one of many that have been taken up by showbiz in its proletarianization of manners.

gill, *n* – a quarter-pint. Used in cooking.

gillie, *n* – an assistant to someone out hunting game,

who loads his shotgun for him. A Scottish word.

gilt-edged, *adj* – refers to government stocks.

gin, *n* – a small trap for animals.

ginger or **ginger up**, *v* – to prod into further action. Also used adjectivally; within a large organization, such as a political party, a group of people will sometimes form a 'ginger' group'.

Girl Guide, *n* – Girl Scout.

Giro, *prop n* – a Post Office and banking service providing money-transfer facilities.

git, *n* (col) – person; a vaguely offensive term. Robert Graves says in his small book *Lars Porsena or The Future of Swearing* that it comes from 'whore's git', i.e. 'whore's begat', but it has lost much of its strength since then.

glasshouse, *n* (col) – a military prison.

glaze, *v* – to fit with glass, as a window. A **glazier** is a person who fits windows.

glow worm, *n* – lightning bug.

gnomes of Zurich, *n* – the international Swiss bankers who supposedly pull strings and manipulate the international monetary system. They figure in British political folklore.

go, *n* – a try, as in 'I'll have a go'.

gob, *n* – mouth; a **gob-stopper** is a huge candy.

gods, *n* (col) – the cheapest seats at the theater, at the back of the top balcony, so-called because they are supposedly close to heaven.

golden handshake, *n* – a

financial payment made to an executive on leaving a firm.

golliwog, *n* – a black-faced doll resembling a black minstrel.

gong, *n* (col) – medal or decoration. Originally service slang.

goods, *n* – freight, as in **goods train**, **goods lift** (elevator), etc.

goolies, *n* – see GHOULIES.

Gorbals, *prop n* – a notoriously rough slum district of Glasgow.

gorblimey!, *interj* – an expression of surprise. It is Cockney, so much so that I've heard someone called 'a real gorblimey Cockney.' It derives from the archaic and blasphemous 'God blind me!'

gormless, *adj* (col) – stupid and unattractive.

governor, *n* – 1. the warden of a prison. 2. (col) boss. Working-class.

governor-general, *n* – the Queen's representative in an independent country in the British Commonwealth, such as Canada and Australia, who signs laws and carries out ceremonials in her place.

grace-and-favour home, *n* – a home on a royal estate given for life to a relative of the royal family or to someone for services to the nation.

gradient, *n* – grade on a road.

graft, *n* (col) – 1. hard work, honest toil. 2. alternatively, almost the opposite, i.e. sharp dealings, such as dishonest sales talk. A *grafter* can be someone who practises either one.

grammar school, *n* – traditionally, the more advanced academically of the two kinds of school into which British

secondary education has been divided, covering roughly the equivalent of the sixth to the twelfth grades. Most of these were abolished in the 1970s as part of the egalitarian schools policy of successive Labour Governments, but the issue is controversial and they could be brought back.

gramophone, *n* – phonograph. Actually, this term is hardly used now, having been replaced by record-player.

grant, *n* – the payment from government funds of a college student's tuition and basic living costs. Every student is entitled to this, according to his or her means (or, more usually, their parents' means).

grass, *n* – someone who gives evidence against criminal confederates. **supergrass** is a term coined recently by newspapers to mean an important informer who brings about the arrest of a lot of criminals.

greaseproof paper, *n* – wax paper.

green belt, *n* – a belt of land around a city where little or no building is permitted.

Green Cross Code, *prop n* – the road safety rules that schoolchildren learn.

green fingers, *n* – green thumbs.

greengage – n – a fruit similar to a plum only green in color.

greengrocer, *n* – someone who sells fruits and vegetables, but not other staple foods. A **grocer** sells these and perhaps fruits and vegetables as well, as in America.

green paper, *n* – a statement of government views or proposals, published as a document for discussion. See also WHITE PAPER.

greens, *n* – green vegetables.

grind, *n* (col) – sexual intercourse. ' "A good grind, eh?" said the tramp, looking after the fräulein.' – from *Love Among the Haystacks* by D. H. Lawrence.

gripewater, *n* – a type of medicine commonly given to babies to help with digestion.

grizzle, *v* – to whine or cry complainingly.

grocer, *n* – dealer in foodstuffs; see GREENGROCER.

grog, *n* – rum and water. Until 1971, a daily ration of grog was given to enlisted men in the Royal Navy. It is used occasionally as a synonym for any liquor.

grotty, *adj* (col) – crummy, shabby. A new word that came out of Liverpool in the Beatles era, it stems from 'grotesque'.

ground floor, *n* – first floor.

groundnut, *n* – peanut. Used only in an agricultural context, e.g. one is not offered a groundnut at a cocktail party, but Jimmy Carter farmed them.

group-captain, *n* – an RAF rank equivalent to a colonel.

Guards, *prop n* – the army division consisting of the five regiments which mount guard outside the Queen's palaces, plus two cavalry regiments which ride in royal processions. These are all fighting units, which perform their palace duties on a rota system.

gubbins, *n* – thingamajig.

guinea, *n* – in pre-1971, pre-decimal coinage, 21 shillings, or one pound one shilling.

gum, *n* – a light glue, used for paper mostly.

gumboots, *n* – see WELLINGTONS.

gun, *n* – sometimes this means a place in a game-shooting group. Advertisements in country-life magazines sometimes begin 'Fourth gun wanted . . .'

gunsmith, *n* – a manufacturer of guns.

Guy Fawkes Night, *prop n* – November 5th, celebrated with bonfires and fireworks, to mark the foiling of a plot to blow up the Houses of Parliament led by Guy Fawkes in 1605. A **guy** is an effigy of Guy Fawkes, traditionally burned on a bonfire on the night.

H

haberdasher, *n* – a seller of notions and small items connected with clothes, such as thread and buttons. He does *not* sell clothes.

hack, *v* – to kick someone deliberately in a game.

hacking jacket, *n* – a riding jacket, with tight waist, slanted pockets with flaps and vents, or a sports jacket that follows this style.

haggis, *n* – a Scottish national dish eaten by no one but Scots; consisting of a sheep's entrails with oats and other things added, sewn up in the lining of a sheep's stomach, to an Englishman an object of awe, distaste and lurid speculation.

ha-ha, *n* – a sunken wall or fence dividing a field, usually a landscaped garden, from the surrounding countryside, so constructed as to give an unimpaired view.

hake, *n* – an edible fish, related to the cod.

half, *adv* – **not half** means very much. 'There wasn't half a row!' means that there was a terrific argument.

half-inch, *v* (col) – to steal, Cockney rhyming slang ('pinch').

hall of residence, *n* – a dormitory building for students. A 'dormitory' in British is always one room where a number of people sleep.

hall porter, *n* – the man in a hotel who rules the bell boys and carries out services for guests. He will not carry your bags.

hard cheese, hard lines, *n* – tough luck. Mostly upper-class.

Harley Street, *prop n* – the area of London where Britain's highest-rated doctors have their offices.

hat-trick, *n* – a cricket term, it means bowling out (an approximate equivalent of striking out) three batsmen (batters) in a row. It is also used outside cricket to mean any string of three successes.

headmaster or **head,** *n* – the principal of a school.

Heinz, *n* (col) – at the racetrack, 57 bets in combination, involving six horses. Obviously from Heinz 57 varieties.

helter skelter, *n* – a spiral slide at a fairground.

High Church, *n* and *adj* – a Church of England style close to Roman Catholicism, with an emphasis on ritual and the Latin liturgy. Sometimes called **Anglo-Catholic.**

high street, *n* – main street, the

principal shopping street of a small town.

high tea, *n* – a late afternoon meal, replacing tea (see TEA) and supper, usually containing some elements of each.

hire, *v* – to rent something from someone. In Britain, you hire a car or a television set. Hertz and Avis rent cars. However, one rents a dwelling place.

hire purchase, *n* – instalment plan.

hive off, *v* – to separate from the main body, e.g. 'They're hiving off the overseas operation and making it a separate company.'

hoarding, *n* – billboard.

hob, *n* – the top of a stove, on which things are cooked.

Hobson's choice, *n* – something presented as a choice, but in which one has no real alternative. As it was explained in 1700, 'Where to elect there is but one,/'Tis Hobson's choice, Take that or none.' – from *England Reformed* by Thomas Ward.

hockey, *n* – field hockey, primarily a girls' sport in Britain.

Hogmanay, *prop n* – a Scottish New Year's Eve, traditionally celebrated with much drink and festivity. One of Evelyn Waugh's characters in *Decline and Fall* defined it deflatingly as 'being sick on Glasgow pavements.' New Year's Eve has always been a bigger occasion in Scotland than in England and Wales. New Year's Day was only made a national holiday in England in 1976, whereas it has always been one in Scotland. The

Scots, saving their celebratory energies for New Year's Eve, do not make as much of Christmas, and until the 1960s December 25 was an ordinary working day in Scotland, a result of the Calvinist disapproval of merry-making on a religious occasion.

hokey cokey, *n* – a kind of urban folk dance.

holdall, *n* – a soft suitcase.

hold-up, *n* – a traffic jam or blockage, often, rather than anything more violent.

Home Counties, *prop n* – the counties that border on London, containing much of exurbia. Often used as a synonym for smart exurbia and its lifestyle.

home help, *n* – a woman sent by the local council to do housework for elderly or infirm people.

homely, *adj* – home-loving, running a good home. Used about someone's appearance, it can mean pleasant and comfortable, and is not necessarily insulting.

Home Office, *prop n* – the government department responsible for law and order and other domestic affairs, including immigration.

Home Secretary, *prop n* – the minister in charge of this department, a senior member of the cabinet.

honorary, *adj* – unpaid. The Hon. Secretary or Hon. Treasurer of an organization is unpaid and doing it in his spare time.

Honourable, *adj* – an honorific applied (but not in speaking to them) to the younger sons of an earl and all the children of a viscount or baron. The term is not applied to Members of Parliament, though when referring to one another in the House they must use it, e.g. 'the Honourable Member for Bashton-under-Lyme'. The Right Honourable is applied to members of the Privy Council (see PRIVY COUNCIL).

honours list, *n* – the roll of those people who receive new titles of nobility and other honours. There are two of these each year, the **New Year Honours,** announced on January 1, and the **Birthday Honours,** on the day in June designated as the Queen's official birthday, which changes from year to year. There is also one when a government resigns and dissolves parliament.

hood, *n* – the soft top of a convertible. A car's hood is a **bonnet** in British.

Hooray Henry, *n* (col) – a young man of pronounced upper-class accent manners and the ways of an overgrown schoolboy. A dismissive term.

hoot, *n* (col) – something funny. 'It's a hoot!' means 'It's a riot!'

hooter, *n* (col) – nose, schnozzle.

hoover, *n* and *v* – a vacuum cleaner. The brand name has come to signify the appliance itself. It is used as a verb, to **hoover.**

hot pot, *n* – a mutton and vegetable stew, a North of England dish.

hounds, *n* – in the singular this could conceivably mean any kind of dog, but in the plural it only means foxhounds, and is used in connection with fox-hunting.

houseman, *n* – an intern in a hospital.

housey housey, *n* – a form of bingo, traditional in the services.

housing development or **housing estate,** *n* – housing project.

hovercraft, *n* – air cushioned vehicle.

HP, *n* (abbr) – see HIRE PURCHASE.

hump, *v* – to carry something heavy.

hump, *n* (col) – a fit of bad temper or annoyance, as in 'he's got the hump'.

hundredweight, *n* – 112 lb, perversely, instead of the American hundredweight's 100 lb.

hunt, *v* – fox-hunting, unless otherwise specified.

Hush Puppy, *prop n* – not, in Britain, something you eat, but a brand-name for a light, soft suede shoe.

I

ice, *n* – ice cream. Both terms are used. 'Ice' also means ice.

icing sugar, *n* – confectionery sugar.

identikit, *n* – the composition of a pictorial likeness of someone by putting together a number of facial characteristics by a particular method. The particular method most used was devised by Hugh C. McDonald of Los Angeles, but it is now used by the British police.

immersion heater, *n* – an apparatus for heating water by immersing it in the water. A tank with one of these is called an immersion tank.

impression, *n* – printing. A publisher will sometimes talk about a first and second impression instead of a first and second printing.

industrial, *adj* – often referring to labor, as in industrial dispute and industrial reporter.

inertia selling, *n* – sending unsolicited goods to people and asking them to pay for them.

infant school, *n* – the first two years of school, covering ages 5–7.

inland, *adj* – domestic, internal, as in Inland Revenue for Internal Revenue.

inquiry agent, *n* – private detective.

instructor, *n* – a teacher in a technical or vocational institution, not a college or university.

inverted commas, *n* – quotation marks.

ironmongery, *n* – hardware. An ironmonger's is a hardware store.

J

jacket potato, *n* – baked potato in its skin.

jelly, *n* – Jello.

jemmy, *n* – jimmy.

jerry, *n* (col) – 1. chamber pot. Dated, as is the object. 2. German. The word comes from the First World War, and derives from the fact that the German army helmet looked like one.

job, *n* – **on the job** means, colloquially, engaged in sexual intercourse. An English friend was delighted when an American told her proudly that his 75-year-old uncle had died on the job.

job centre, *n* – a government-run employment exchange.

joiner, *n* – a carpenter who does small often delicate domestic work.

joinery, *n* – woodwork.

joint, *n* – a piece of meat for roasting. The **Sunday joint** is a household tradition.

joint, *v* – in cooking, to disjoint.

jolly, *n* (col) – a party, or jolly get-together.

judge's rules, *n* – the rules governing the treatment of an arrested man by the police.

judy, *n* – girl. Working-class.

juggernaut, *n* – a very large truck.

jumble sale, *n* – rummage sale.

jumper, *n* – a light pullover.

junction, *n* – intersection.

junior school, *n* – the second phase of school, covering ages 7–11.

K

karsi, *n* (col) – toilet. Cockney. Pronounced 'karzi'.

kedgeree, *n* – a dish made of rice and shredded fish.

kerfuffle, *n* (col) – a row or disturbance.

kettle, *n* – tea kettle. Any other kind is a pot or casserole dish in Britain. The one culinary exception is a **fish kettle**, a long, narrow utensil for boiling fish. Hence the expression, when something is fouled up, 'That's a fine kettle of fish!'

khyber, *n* (col) – fanny. Rhyming slang: Khyber Pass – arse (they rhyme if you pronounce 'pass' as the British do).

kip, *n* (col) – a sleep.

kipper, *n* – kippered (dried and smoked) herring, a popular breakfast food.

Kirby grips, *prop n* – bobby pins. A trade name.

kiss of life, *n* – mouth-to-mouth resuscitation.

kite mark, *n* – a kite-shaped mark on a manufactured item that indicates that it meets the requirements of the British Standards Institute.

knacker, *n* – a horse slaughterer. A **knacker's yard** is the place where horses are slaughtered.

knackered, *adj* (col) – tired-out. Originally a country term, it meant, applied to an animal, emasculated.

knees-up, *n* (col) – party. Mostly Cockney or mock-Cockney. 'Knees up Mother Brown' is a song often sung and danced to on such occasions in traditional working-class neighborhoods.

knee trembler, *n* (col) – sexual intercourse standing up.

knickers, *n* – old-fashioned women's underpants, like bloomers.

knighthood, *n* – one of several honors bestowed for services to the nation. They all carry the title 'Sir', and none is hereditary.

knocking shop, *n* – brothel.

knock off, *v* (col) – steal.

knock-on, *adj* – a **knock-on effect** is a follow-on effect, one that occurs subsequently to the first one.

knock up, *v* – 1. to wake or rouse someone. (See entry in American/British section.) 2. to make something quickly, such as a meal or a home-made piece of furniture.

knock-up, *n* – knocking a ball about before starting a game, as in tennis.

L

labourer, *n* – an unskilled outdoor workman, on a farm or construction site.

Labour Party, *prop n* – one of the two main political parties in Britain, it covers a wide spectrum of opinion from the center leftwards. It was founded in 1900 to give labor unions a voice in parliament, and the unions are still corporate members, but it is an independent party and far from being simply the voice of organized labor.

lacquer, *n* – any ordinary hair spray.

ladder, *n* – a run in hose or stockings.

Lady, *n* – a form of address which usually prefixes the name of a countess, marchioness, viscountess, or baroness, the wife of a baronet or a knight, and the daughter of a duke, marquess, or earl. In the last-named cases, the title precedes the first name, e.g. Lady Jane Bigglesworth.

ladybird, *n* – ladybug.

lag, *n* (col) – a long-time occupant of prisons. Always called an **old lag**.

lager, *n* – a light beer, with a more sophisticated appeal than the more widely consumed bitter. See BITTER.

lamp-post, *n* – street lamp.

Lancashire hot pot, *n* – a meat-and-potatoes stew.

lance corporal, *n* – the first army rank above a buck private.

landlord, *n* – pub-keeper. Same as LICENSEE (see).

lashings, *n* – large servings of food or drink, e.g. 'roast beef, with lashings of Yorkshire pudding and gravy'.

lavatory, *n* – toilet.

lay, *v* – of the table, to set the table.

layabout, *n* – a loafer, someone who does not work.

lay-by, *n* – a pull-off on a freeway.

lay on, *v* – to organize, arrange. A tourist guide might tell a party that 'lunch and a visit to the castle are laid on for today'.

leader or **leading article,** *n* – an editorial in a newspaper.

lead-swinging or (sometimes) **swinging the lead,** *adj* (col) – gold-bricking. Sometimes shortened to 'swinging it'. The term has a nautical derivation; the sailor charged with taking soundings with a lead and line might be found swinging it idly, instead of doing his job.

left luggage office, *n* – checkroom.

legal aid, *n* – payment from

government funds for legal services for someone who cannot afford it himself, a feature of Britain's welfare system.

level crossing, *n* – railroad crossing.

Liberal Jew, *n* – a Jew roughly similar to a Reform Jew in America in the degree of his deviation from orthodoxy. Jewish religious practise in Britain is divided into three streams, from right to left Orthodox, Reform and Liberal.

Liberal Party, *prop n* – this was one of the two major parties for more than a century, but its role as the party of the left was taken over by the Labour Party in the 1920s and it has dwindled in size and importance. Ideologically, it stands between the Labour and Conservative parties.

liberty, *n* – cheek, impudence. He's got a liberty!' means 'He's got a nerve!'

licensed, *adj* – licensed to serve liquor.

licensee, *n* – the manager of a pub, the person who holds the license to run it.

licensing laws, *n* – the laws governing when and where liquor may be sold. Excise laws cover only taxation and import.

lido, *n* – outdoor swimming pool.

lie-in, *n* – a rest in bed in the morning.

life peer, *n* – someone who has been given the title of baron or baroness and an accompanying seat in the House of Lords, which are for life only and are not passed on to the descendants. This new form of nobleman was created by an Act of Parliament in 1958.

lift, *n* – elevator.

light ale, *n* – pale ale, usually slightly sweeter than other light beers.

limited or **Ltd,** *adj* – incorporated. It stands for 'limited liability'.

lines, *n* – a punishment commonly given to a child at school, of having to write out fifty or so times some line like 'I must not throw things in class'.

line shoot, *n* (col) – a boastful tale; to **shoot a line** is to exaggerate or fabricate one's exploits or position. From Second World War RAF slang.

lip-salve, *n* – chap-stick. One American says that when he asked his hotel porter in London where he could get a chap-stick, he was directed to a Chinese restaurant.

living, *n* – in the Church of England, the tenure of office of a parson, originally resulting from a donation.

loaf, *n* (col) – head, brains. It is Cockney rhyming slang: loaf of bread – head.

lobby correspondent, *n* – the political correspondent of a newspaper, so-called because he is a member of the small group of journalists who are allowed into the Members' lobby of the House of Commons.

local, *n* (col) – the particular pub that is an Englishman's meeting place, and sometimes home from home. He might say, 'The Volunteer Arms is my local, which one do you use?'

locum, *n* – a doctor or lawyer substituting for another during a temporary absence. Short for *locum tenens*, Latin for 'holder of the place'.

lodger, *n* – roomer.

logic-chopping, *v* – academic hair-splitting.

lollipop man, *n* – a man who escorts children across the road outside a school, so-called because he carries a pole with a large circular sign on the end, shaped like a lollipop.

lolly, *n* (col) – money.

long johns, *n* – men's long-legged underpants.

long jump, *n* – broad jump.

long stop, *n* – a term from cricket, it means a person or institution that serves to block something undesirable if it gets through every other obstacle. 'Many bills are sent to the House of Lords so late that it cannot be expected to act as an efficient long stop.' – article in the (London) *Times*.

long vac, *n* – the 3$\frac{1}{2}$-month mid-year vacation from Oxford and Cambridge and some other universities.

loo, *n* (col) – toilet. A genteel colloquialism, this.

loofah, *n* – a kind of bath scrubber made from the loofah plant.

look-out, *n* – outlook. Both terms are used.

Lord, *n* – a form of address to any male peer below a duke. One never speaks in Britain of 'a lord'.

Lord Chancellor, *prop n* – the head of the judiciary, who is ex officio speaker of the House of Lords and a member of the cabinet.

Lord Lieutenant, *n* – an office-holder, usually a nobleman, who in theory holds powers in an area deputed by the monarch, but whose functions in fact are largely ceremonial. Pronounced 'lord leftenant'.

Lord Privy Seal, *prop n* – an office with duties that are now obsolete retained so as to give some leading politician a title that carries with it a position in the cabinet, as a kind of minister without portfolio.

Lord's, *prop n* – Britain's principal cricket stadium, in London.

Lords, the, *prop n* – the House of Lords, the upper house of parliament, though much less important politically than the House of Commons. It consists of most peers (barons and upwards) whether their title is hereditary or conferred for life only, plus the leaders of the Church of England.

lorry, *n* – truck.

loud-hailer, *n* – bull-horn.

lounge suit, *n* – an ordinary man's suit. It was called this in the last century to distinguish it from formal wear, and the term has remained.

low church, *n* and *adj* – a Church of England style that is very Protestant, emphasizing simplicity and direct participation in the service.

L-plate, *n* – 'L' sign on a car signifying that the driver is still learning. It is required by law.

lucky dip, *n* – grab bag.

ludo, *n* – a common children's

game with board, dice and counters.

lug-hole, *n* (col) – ear.

lumber, *v* – to make someone do a job, or handle the situation, e.g. 'Everyone else was going on holiday so they lumbered me with it.' Very much used in the reflexive: there was a popular song called 'I've Been Lumbered.'

lumber room, *n* – a spare room where things are stored.

lump, *n* – casual, non-union building workers. They have been dubbed **the lump,** collectively, by regular workers in the trade; the word comes from *lumpenproletariat.*

lump, *v* (col) – to accept unwillingly, but without much choice. 'Like it or lump it' is a common saying.

luncheon voucher, *n* – a voucher, given by some employers to staff in addition to salary, which can be exchanged for food in a restaurant.

M

mackintosh or **mac**, *n* – rain-coat. The first is becoming less common, the abbreviation is still much used.

magic, *adj* (col) – marvellous, excellent. A Scottish word that has traveled south in the past few years.

mains, *n* – the electricity supply. For instance, an electrical device may be said to work off 'mains or battery'.

maisonette, *n* – a duplex apart-ment, often part of a house.

managing director, *n* – the chief executive officer of a corpora-tion.

Mancunian, *n* – a citizen of Manchester.

manse, *n* – the home of a mini-ster of the Church of Scotland, a term redolent of frugality, asceticism and high principles.

Manx, *adj* – pertaining to the Isle of Man, a small island off northwest England. A **Manx cat** is a breed of tail-less cat.

marching orders, *n* – walking papers.

market garden, *n* – truck farm.

marriage lines, *n* – marriage certificate.

marrow, *n* – a native vegetable, a kind of squash.

Martini, *prop n* – a popular brand of vermouth, often drunk straight as an aperitif. If you ask simply for 'martini' at most British pubs, you are likely to be given a glass of vermouth rather than a cock-tail. Even prefixing it with 'dry' may get you only a dry vermouth.

mash, *n* (col) – mashed potatoes.

mason, *n* – a worker in stone, never, as in America, in brick as well.

Master, *n* – the equivalent title to Mr to a boy child. Its use is very formal.

mate, *n* – friend, pal. Working-class.

maths, *n* – math.

Mayfair, *prop n* – the smart, rich district in the center of London.

mayor, *n* – the chairman of a municipal or borough council, whose activities outside the council chamber are cere-monial. He does not have the executive power of an American mayor, nor is he elected directly.

may tree, *n* – a hawthorn tree (but the British use 'hawthorn bush').

MBE, *n* (abbr) – Member, Order of the British Empire, an honor awarded for many kinds of services to the nation.

mean, *adj* – stingy, tight with

money. It does not usually mean nasty in the more general sense.

Meccano, *prop n* – the most popular boys' construction set, similar to an Erector set.

mental, *adj* (col) – mentally ill, insane.

MEP, *n* (abbr) – member of the European Parliament.

merchant bank, *n* – investment bank.

Messrs – an abbreviation of 'Messieurs', a formal mode of address often used in business correspondence to a firm, e.g. 'Messrs Bloggs, Blunt and Bottomley, solicitors . . .'

methylated spirits, *n* – similar to wood alcohol. A **meths drinker** is an alcoholic bum reduced to drinking this.

Metropolitan Police, *prop n* – the London police.

mews, *n* – an alley, often a very fashionable one, that used to contain stables for horses and living space for the grooms and other staff above, and now consists of town houses or apartments, sometimes with garages where the stables were. There is, in fact, at least one mews in New York City; Washington Mews, near Washington Square.

MFH, *n* – master of foxhounds, the man who directs a regular fox hunt and sets its standards, a position of some social standing.

MI5, *n* – the domestic intelligence, or counter-espionage service. The initials stood originally for 'Military Intelligence'.

MI6, *n* – the intelligence service that operates overseas, roughly equivalent to the CIA. Within the government this is called the **SIS**, or **Secret Intelligence Service**, but MI6 is the term used by the public. The government won't correct anyone since it will rarely admit that any such organizations exist.

mick, *n* (col) – an Irishman. A neutral term, quite acceptable to Irishmen.

mickey, *n* (col) – to **take the mickey out of** someone means to make fun of him.

Midlands, *prop n* – central England.

mild, *n* – mild ale, a dark-colored ale with less hop flavoring than light ale. **mild and bitter** used to be a favorite drink, but as pubs change, it is seen less.

milk float, *n* – a small dairy delivery truck.

mills bomb, *n* – a First World War hand grenade.

minced meat or **mince**, *n* – hamburger meat.

mineral water, *n* – any carbonated soft drink.

mingy, *adj* – meagre, scanty.

mini-cab, *n* – a car that serves as a taxi in answer to calls, but is not licensed to cruise for fares.

minim, *n* – half-note. Musical.

mistress, *n* – a member of the teaching staff in a girls' school. When, during the Second World War, the RAF took over a famous girls' boarding school called Roedean to billet trainee pilots, the new arrivals found next to every bed a button and a notice saying: 'If you want a mistress during the night, ring the bell.' The first night was bedlam, so the story goes.

mix, *v* (col) – to cause dissension, such as by spreading false tales. A **mixer** is someone who makes trouble in this way. To **mix it** sometimes means to row or fight.

mixed grill, *n* – a dish of several kinds of grilled meat with mushrooms and tomatoes.

mob, *n* (col) – apart from its literal meaning of an angry crowd, this means a group of people in a much less pejorative sense than in America. 'Our mob' means something like 'our gang', and a man will speak of his outfit in the army as his mob.

moggy, *n* – pet cat.

moleskin, *n* – a rough cotton fabric.

momentarily, *adv* – for a short time. This is different from the common (although strictly speaking, erroneous) American use, to mean very soon, *in* a short time. Pointing up the difference, one Nicholas Lane, a Briton living in Pittsburgh, wrote recently that when he is travelling by air in America, 'Every time a stewardess tells me that my plane will take off momentarily, I have visions of kangaroo-hopping across the country.'

monkey, *n* (col) – £500.

monkey nuts, *n* – peanuts in their shells.

moonlight flit, *n* (col) – a departure by night to avoid paying rent that is owed.

moor, *n* – an area of flat, rough, open country.

moped, *n* – a mini-bike, a low-powered motorcycle.

Moss Bros, *prop n* – not the author's two sons, but a London firm which hires out clothes, particularly evening dress. The name has become another term for hired finery – 'You're wearing your Moss Bros tonight, I see' – and the subject of innumerable jokes. Usually pronounced 'Moss Bross'.

MOT, *n* – Ministry of Transport. Used about a car, it means that it has passed the Ministry's road-worthiness test.

motorist, *n* – car driver. A newspaper's **motoring correspondent** covers the automobile industry.

motorway, *n* – superhighway. The big motorways in Britain are called M1, M2, and so on.

mouth organ, *n* – harmonica.

MP, *n* – Member of Parliament; actually, of the House of Commons, the elected house. The letters are put after a member's name, e.g. John Smith, MP.

Mr, *n* (abbr) – as well as an ordinary form of address, this is also given to a doctor or dentist who has attained the rank of surgeon. Americans going for medical treatment in Britain have sometimes drawn back when they found the practitioner described as 'Mr So-and-so', and said they wanted to see a qualified doctor. In fact, he would be a doctor of elevated status.

Mrs Mop, *n* (col) – a cleaning lady.

muck about, *v* (col) – to mess about.

mucker, *n* (col) – friend. Very working-class.

muck in, *v* (col) – to pitch in together.

mufti, *adj* – civilian clothes, as distinct from a uniform.

mug, *n* – sucker. A **mug's game** is something which cannot be profitable.

muggins, *n* (col) – a sucker. Usually used without the article, e.g. 'I was muggins'.

mug up, *v* – to study something intensely, read up on.

mum, *n* (col) – mom, ma.

mushy peas, *n* – peas that have been cooked and processed, so that they collapse into a mush.

music-hall, *n* – vaudeville.

muslin, *n* – cheesecloth.

mustard pickle, *n* – cucumbers pickled in mustard sauce.

muzzy, *adj* – woozy, befuddled.

N

Naafi, *n* (abbr) – a canteen for servicemen, the British PX. An acronym of Army, Navy and Air Force Institute.

naff, *adj* (col) – dreary, and socially unacceptable. A new word that may or may not last.

naff off!, *v* (col) – Beat it! Used only in the imperative. It is associated with Princess Anne, who issued it as a kind of royal command to Press photographers whose proximity was interfering with her horsemanship.

nana, *n* (col) – fool. Working-class.

nancy or **nancy boy,** *n* – homosexual.

nap, *n* – a strong tip. To **go nap** on something means to stake a lot on it.

nappy, *n* – diaper.

nark, *n* (col) – police informer.

narky, *adj* (col) – short-tempered, snappy. Dated. **narked** means irritated, annoyed.

National Insurance, *n* – the scheme of compulsory government insurance, part of the premium being paid by the employee and part by his employer.

national service, *n* – peace-time conscription, abolished in Britain in 1958; service as a peace-time conscript, e.g. 'I was doing my national service'.

naturalization papers, *n* – citizenship papers.

navvy, *n* – an unskilled workman on roadwork. The word originated in the first part of the nineteenth century, when it was applied to the men who dug the navigational canals that criss-crossed Britain.

nearside, *adj* – in driving, this refers to the side of the car nearest the edge of the road. In Britain this is the left side, in America the right. The opposite is **offside**.

neat, *adj* – straight, of a drink, e.g. 'neat whisky' is straight whisky.

neck, *n* (col) – nerve, cheek. Churchill used the word to powerful effect in a pun famous during World War II. In a speech after the end of the Battle of Britain, he recalled a forecast by defeatist French generals that Britain would 'have her neck wrung like a chicken'. After a heavy pause, he added: 'Some chicken . . . Some neck!' This was greeted with a roar of applause, and the phrase was repeated often and gleefully by Britons.

needle, *n* (col) – ill-will or a grudge, e.g. 'He's got the needle,' or 'that gives me the needle'.

nervy, *adj* – nervous, jumpy; almost the opposite of the American meaning.

never-never, *n* (col) – instalment plan, as in 'she bought it on the never-never'.

news reader, *n* – a TV news announcer.

new town, *n* – a town built up from scratch as government policy near London or some other urban center to take the overspill.

nib, *n* – a pen point, other than a ball-point.

nick, *v* (col) – to steal.

nick, *n* (col) – 1. prison. 2. police station. 3. condition of an article, e.g. 'a 10-year-old car, but it's in good nick'.

nightdress, *n* – nightgown.

nip, *v* – to go briefly, e.g. 'I'll just nip down to the corner.'

nipper, *n* (col) – child, kid.

nipple, *n* – this means *only* the nipple on a woman's breast (or man's chest), never on a baby's bottle; this is a teat. Dr Benjamin Spock, in his *Baby and Child Care*, a book which has had as wide circulation in Britain as in America, suggests that if a baby has difficulty in feeding, it may be an idea to widen the hole in the nipple by inserting a sharp needle. This has caused some confusion and much wincing among young British mothers, but so far as is known, no physical injury.

nippy, *adj* (col) – snappy, quick.

Nissen hut, *n* – quonset hut.

nit, *n* – fool.

nob, *n* (col) – big shot, someone of high standing. British visi-

tors to San Francisco assume that this is how Nob Hill got its name.

nobble, *v* (col) – to get at and influence or persuade, e.g. 'He tried to nobble some members of the inquiry board'. In racing (and sometimes other contests), it means to dope or injure a horse (or other contestant).

nod, *n* – **on the nod** means accepted without argument or formal debate. If a committee passes a motion on the nod, it means that no formal vote was taken and it was passed by common assent.

Noddy, *prop n* – A little boy in a gnome-like hat in tiny tots' stories. It sometimes stands for toyland.

noggin, *n* – an alcoholic drink.

no-go, *adj* – restricted, not to be entered without permission.

nonconformist, *adj* – a Protestant church that is not in communion with the Church of England, such as the Baptist or Presbyterian.

Norfolk Broads, *prop n* – not the local girls, but a low-lying area of Norfolk with interconnected stretches of water, area of Norfolk with interconOften called just 'the Broads'.

Norman, *adj* – pertaining to the period after the Norman Conquest of England in 1066.

nosey parker, *n* – busybody.

nosh, nosh-up, *n* (col) – a new and voguish word in Britain, it means food and in particular, a slap-up meal. It has changed meaning in coming over from Yiddish-American, where it means a bite or snack.

note, *n* – a Treasury bill. One

speaks of a 'pound note', not bill.

not half, *adj* (col) – see HALF.

noughts and crosses, *n* – tic tac toe.

nous, *n* (col) – rhyming with 'mouse', savvy, intelligence in a particular situation.

number plate, *n* – similar to a license plate on a car.

nursing home, *n* – a private hospital.

nut, *n* – 1. of butter, a knob of butter. 2. (col) to **do one's nut** is to become frantic, e.g. 'If the boss hears about this he'll do his nut.'

nutter, *n* (col) – a crazy person.

O

oast house, *n* – a building containing a kiln for drying the hops or malt used in making beer. It has a roof in the shape of a sloping cone, a feature of the countryside in some parts of England.

OBE, *n* (abbr) – the Order of the British Empire, awarded for many kinds of service to the nation. The letters, as the initials of other decorations or orders of chivalry, are put after a person's name.

OCTU, *n* (abbr) – Officer Cadet Training School.

odds-on, *n* and *adj* – better than even odds. A horse running at 5–6 is the odds-on favorite.

off, *adj* – spoiled, of food, e.g. 'The fridge is broken and the fish and milk are off.'

off-licence, *n* – liquor store. The term comes from its license to sell liquor for consumption off the premises.

offside, *adj* – in driving, the side of the car away from the sidewalk. The opposite is **nearside.**

off-the-peg, *adj* – ready-made, of clothes.

oilskins, *n* – oilers.

Old Bailey, *prop n* – the principal London criminal court.

Old Bill, *prop n* (col) – the Old Bill is the police.

old boy, *n* – an old grad, or alumnus. A school has an old boys' reunion, not an alumni reunion. Similarly, **old girls** are alumnae.

old boy network, *n* – the supposed system by which people of the same upper-class school background extend mutual help in getting ahead.

Old Contemptibles, *prop n* – veterans of the British Army that went to France in 1914 in the early months of the First World War, or often, more loosely, of the First World War army. The term comes from a remark of the Kaiser's. He termed the 1914 British Expeditionary Force a 'contemptible little army', an opinion he was soon to change. Characteristically, the British soldiers took this up as a sobriquet, and bore it proudly.

old rope, *n* (col) – something worthless. 'Money for old rope', a common phrase, means money for jam.

O-levels, *n* – a series of important exams taken at age fifteen or sixteen.

OM, *n* (abbr) – Order of Merit. An award given by the nation for exceptional life-long achievement. Members of the order are limited to twenty-four, plus the occasional foreign member. The last American member was General Eisenhower.

on-camera – in television, a stand-up piece.

one-off, *n* – something devised for use only once or to stand on its own. For instance, a TV documentary may be one of a series or else a one-off.

one-over-the-eight, *adj* – drunk.

o.n.o., *n* (abbr) – or nearest offer. Seen often in ads, e.g. 'For sale, £150 o.n.o. . . .'

open-cast mining, *n* – strip mining.

opening time, *n* – the time at which pubs may open and sell drinks, about 11.30 in the morning and 6.00 in the evening, varying slightly by districts.

Open University, *prop n* – a national university with correspondence courses, aided by radio and TV programs, to enable people to earn a degree at home.

operating theatre, *n* – operating room in a hospital.

oppo, *n* (col) – close companion. Working-class.

ordinary shares, *n* – common stock.

Ordnance Survey, *prop n* – the official maps of Britain produced by the government.

ostler, *n* – hostler.

other ranks, *n* – servicemen and women other than commissioned officers.

outfitter's or **men's outfitter's,** *n* – haberdasher's.

outsize, *adj* – extra-large, of clothes. A term much used by stores, to break it to the customer gently.

overdraft, *n* – money drawn from a bank in excess of the amount deposited, but usually with the bank's consent. Having an overdraft is a way of borrowing money.

overspill, *n* – an excess of people. An overspill meeting is one that takes those who could not find places in the main one. An overspill town draws surplus population from an urban conurbation.

Oxbridge, *prop n* – a compound of the names of Britain's two senior universities, Oxford and Cambridge, Britain's two senior universi- 'Oxbridge graduates no longer predominate among diplomatic service entrants . . .' – from a report in the (London) *Times*.

Oxonian, *adj* – pertaining to Oxford University.

P

PA, *n* (abbr) – personal assistant.

packet, *n* (col) – a lot of money.

pack up, *v* – break down, stop functioning. A business or a TV set can pack up.

paddle-steamer, *n* – a side-wheeler.

paddy, *n* (col) – 1. an Irishman, usually an Irish workman. 2. a state of high emotion or excitement. 'Don't get in such a paddy!' means 'Cool down'.

paddy wagon, *n* – black maria.

page three, *n* (col) – standing alone, this signifies a semi-nude pin-up. The *Sun*, the British tabloid bought by the international newspaper proprietor Rupert Murdoch, was the first British newspaper to carry photographs of topless girls; it featured them prominently, and does still, on page three.

Pakky, *n* (col) – a Pakistani immigrant. Also spelt Paki.

palais, *n* – a dance hall. They are often called Palais de Danse. Pronounced the French way with a silent 's'.

pale ale, *n* – light ale, light in color and body.

palm court, *n* – a hotel lounge decorated with potted palms. Popular in the 1920s and 30s, the phrase is often used to denote that kind of atmos-phere; **palm court music** is the kind of soupy, romantic, string music played by a palm court orchestra.

pancake, *n* – crepe. It is thinner than an American pancake and is usually eaten for a dessert.

panda car, *n* – police patrol car.

panel, *n* – a doctor's list of National Health Service patients.

pantechnicon, *n* – a furniture removal truck.

pantomine, *n* – a traditional stylized Christmas entertainment for children. It is based loosely on one of the well-known nursery stories, and its special features are songs, spectacle, a hero played by a girl (the **principal boy**) and a comic old woman played by a man (the **dame**). Sometimes shortened to **panto.** A few of these traditions are abandoned in modern productions.

pants, *n* – underpants. Pants are **trousers.**

paraffin, *n* – kerosene.

paralytic, *adj* (col) – blind drunk.

parish, *n* – the district covered by a church in the Church of England; also a rural civil administrative district that is usually the same.

parish pump, *n* and *adj* – parochial, village-minded, referring to the gossip of women around the pump where they used to go for their water, e.g. **parish pump politics.**

parky, *adj* (col) – sharp, biting, referring to the weather.

part exchange, *n* – trade-in.

pasty or **patty,** *n* – a small meat pie.

patch, *n* (col) – one's area or territory, or, if used about a policeman, his beat. An announcement of a forthcoming TV program in the (London) *Sunday Times,* September 18, 1983 'I Remember Harlem. William Miles, black, Harlem-born producer-director, recalls his home patch.'

patience, *n* – the game of solitaire. In Britain, solitaire is a game for one, or sometimes two, played with marbles on a board.

pavement, *n* – sidewalk.

PAYE, *prop n* (abbr) – Pay As You Earn, the system of taxation in which the tax is deducted from wages at source.

PC, *n* (abbr) – police constable. A policeman on the beat is identified as PC ——, followed by the number.

Pearly King/Queen, *n* – a leader in a community of pushcart peddlars who, in accordance with tradition, covers his/her clothes with mother-of-pearl buttons.

pease pudding, *n* – a dish made with peas, usually served with ham or bacon.

pecker, *n* – spirits, courage, used in the phrase 'Keep your pecker up'. In the American/British section, Britons are warned against using this phrase loosely in America. Originally it meant beak, coming, presumably, from the farmyard (the thing a bird pecks with), and 'Keep your pecker up' meant 'Keep your chin up'.

peckish, *adj* – a little hungry.

peer, *n* – someone of noble rank.

peppercorn rent, *n* – a purely nominal rent. It dates from the day when the nominal rent paid to a feudal lord was one peppercorn per year.

perished, *adj* – worn-out, exhausted. A **perisher** is a bout of very bad weather, or an old-fashioned word for a kid.

Perspex, *prop n* – similar to Plexiglass. A trade name.

petrol, *n* – gasoline.

petty cash, *n* – the small amount of cash kept in an office for trivial purchases, such as coffee and paper clips.

petty sessions, *n* – a magistrate's court where minor cases are heard.

pi, *adj* (col) – virtuous, pious, or seeming to be so. Usually derogatory. Mostly upper-class.

pick-axe, *n* – pick.

pick-me-up, *n* – pick-up, in the sense of a reviver.

pie, *n* – often, this has a meat or savoury filling, and is the main course of a meal, served with vegetables. If it is a dessert, it is usually a **deep-dish pie.** The other kind is called a **flan.**

pillar box, *n* – the standard box for mailing letters, usually red and cylindrical.

pillock, *n* (col) – idiot. Juvenile, and newish.

pinch, *v* (col) – 1. to steal; a lightweight word, like 'swipe.' 2. arrest.

pink gin, *n* – gin and bitters, sometimes with water.

pint, *n* – 1. 34.68 cubic inches, slightly larger than an American (liquid) pint. 2. used by itself, colloquially, it means a pint of beer, the standard large-sized beer served in pubs, e.g. 'Let's go and have a pint.'

pip, *v* – to beat by a very small margin. 'US Star Pips Wells. Alan Wells missed a bronze medal by 3/100ths of a second at the World Athletics Championships in Helsinki yesterday.' – headline and report in the *Guardian* newspaper, August 9, 1983.

pip, *v* – 'It gives me the pip' means it annoys me, makes me angry.

pissed, *adj* (col) – drunk.

piss off, *v* (col) – scram.

piss-up, *n* (col) – a drunken party.

pitch, *n* – the ground on which soccer or cricket is played.

place, *v* – at the race track, to come in second or third.

plaice, *n* – a North Sea white fish, a popular food.

plaits, *n* – braids.

platelayer, *n* – tracklayer on the railroad.

platform, *n* – track in a railroad station. A sign will direct passengers to platform 1, 2, etc.

play up, *v* – to act so as to cause trouble. A child or an automobile may play up.

PLC, *n* (abbr) – this stands for 'public limited company', and is the equivalent of 'Inc.' it is replacing **Ltd.**

plimsolls, *n* – sneakers.

plonk, *n* (col) – cheap wine. A genial term, which does not insult the drink.

plough, *v* – to fail in exams, at university. The verb is transitive: an examiner ploughs a student, a student is ploughed.

PLR, *n* (abbr) – **Public Lending Right**, a scheme by which authors receive payment based on the use of their books by public libraries.

PM, *n* (abbr) – Prime Minister.

po, *n* – chamber pot. This word is dropping out of use.

po-faced, *adj* (col) – with an uptight face, solemn and expressionless.

point, *n* – 1. an electric outlet. Also **power point**. 2. on the railroad, a switch.

point duty, *n* – a policeman's traffic duty.

poke, *v* (col) – to screw, have sexual intercourse with, brusquely.

polka dots, *n* – chocolate chips. They would know this in a food store, but it is not widely used. Nobody would understand 'chocolate chips'.

polytechnic, *n* – an institute of higher education that does not have the status of a university nor, normally, any resident students.

ponce, *n* – pimp. To **ponce about** is to saunter showily.

pong, *n* and *v* (col) – smell, odor, e.g. 'After a few months it began to pong a bit.'

pontoon, *n* – another name for the card game blackjack, or twenty-one.

pony, *n* (col) – £25.

pools, *n* – short for football pools, a weekly contest to predict the results of the Saturday soccer matches, in which there are big money prizes. Some five million people fill in pools coupons regularly.

poorly, *adj* (col) – unwell. Old-fashioned, working-class, mostly Northern.

pop, *v* (col) – to go, or put, with small effort, e.g. 'I'll just pop next door,' or 'Pop it in the oven half an hour before dinner-time.'

poppet, *n* – honey, sweetie. A term of endearment. Mostly a woman's word.

porridge, *n* – 1. oatmeal. 2. (col) time served in prison. Long an underworld term, this has now surfaced with a comedy TV series about prison with this title.

porter, *n* – a doorman. In a market, someone who carries produce. It also has the American meaning of someone who carries bags.

posh, *adj* – ultra-smart, high-toned. Though this word has crossed the Atlantic, it is worth including here, first because it is still much more British than American, and second because *Webster's Dictionary* says its origin is unknown. Actually, it dates back to the heyday of Britain's Eastern empire, and is popularly believed to be an acronym of 'port out, starboard home'. On the ships taking Britain's imperial officials and their families to the Far East, the most sought-after and most expensive cabins

were on the port side of the ship on the way out and the starboard side on the way home, because these were the ones most shielded from the strong sun.

post, *n* and *v* – mail. Also **postman, post bag,** etc. 'Mail' is used often for mail that travels long distances, so that one has **air mail** and a **mail train.**

post code, *n* – zip code.

poste restante, *n* – to be held at the post office for collection.

posting, *n* – an assignment for a considerable duration. In the foreign service and the services, for instance, they speak of a posting abroad, or of being posted.

potman, *n* – the man who collects the glasses and cleans up in a pub.

potty, *adj* (col) – crazy.

pouf, pouffe, *n* – 1. a stuffed stool, a hassock. 2. (col) a homosexual.

power point, *n* – see POINT.

pram, *n* – baby carriage.

prang, *v* and *n* (col) – to crash, or damage in an accident; a crash. RAF slang.

prawn, *n* – a large shrimp.

prefect, *n* – a monitor, a pupil chosen to help enforce school discipline.

preggers, *adj* (col) – pregnant. See CHAMPERS.

preliminary hearing, *n* – a hearing before a magistrate to decide whether there is a case to answer. Similar to a grand jury hearing, only there is no jury.

premium bond, *n* – a government bond for one pound sterling that carries no interest, but instead a chance to win a big-money prize in a lottery.

prep, *n* – homework. Upper-class.

prep school, *n* – a private school with the social status of a public school (British) but taking boys or girls at pre-public school age, that is, up to thirteen.

presenter, *n* – on television, an anchor person, or, in an entertainment show, an emcee.

presently, *adv* – soon.

press gang, *n* and *v* – two centuries ago, this was the group of sailors who used to force people into the navy. Now the term is used as a verb and metaphorically; someone may say he was 'press ganged into' doing something.

prezzy, *n* (col) – present, gift.

primary school, *n* – grade school, up to the age of eleven.

primus stove, *n* – a portable kerosene stove.

principal boy, *n* – one of the stars of a pantomime (see PANTOMIME), a girl playing a young man.

prise, *v* – to pry, as in pry open.

Privy Council, *n* – the group of ministers, former ministers and others who traditionally advised the monarch. As a group they still have some constitutional functions.

Privy Purse, *n* – the money voted by parliament for the personal expense of the monarch.

probe, *n* – a dental explorer, the sharp implement with which a dentist explores someone's mouth for cavities.

proctor, *n* – the official at the older universities in charge of discipline of students.

professor, *n* – usually, the chairman of a department at a university. There is usually only one professor to a department, and no such thing as an assistant professor, so the title is a rarer distinction in Britain than in America.

promenade concerts or **proms,** *n* – concerts at which some of the audience stand in the concert hall. The annual season of classical music proms at the Albert Hall in London is a long, strong tradition, particularly among young people.

provinces, *n* – all of Britain outside London, e.g. 'The play had an 8-week tour in the provinces before coming to London.'

provo, *n* – a member of the Provisional IRA, the most active IRA body. It was formed in 1969, soon after the present bout of civil strife started, as a breakaway from the official IRA, which was then dominated by Marxists. The 'officials' are a much smaller and less significant group.

provost, *n* – the mayor of a Scottish city. See MAYOR.

pseud, *n* (col) – someone with unjustified intellectual or artistic pretensions.

publican, *n* – the manager of a pub, rather than the kind of person coupled with sinners in the New Testament.

public bar, *n* – one of the two or three bars in most pubs, the cheaper by a very small amount.

public school, *n* – a private school, which takes boys or girls from the age of thirteen onwards, usually a boarding school; these have a social as well as an educational status. Almost none are co-educational, although some boys' schools now take girls in their senior year.

pukka, *adj* – genuine, sound. An Anglo-Indian word, usually used in an imperial atmosphere, or else for comic effect.

pull or **pull in,** *v* (col) – to pick up successfully a member of the opposite sex. 'Lucy was blonde and broad-hipped and as tempting as an apple, and she could pull any fellow just by giving him the eyelash.' – from *The Little Drummer Girl* by John le Carré.

punchball, *n* – a punching bag.

punch-up, *n* (col) – a fight.

punnet, *n* – a small basket for fruit.

punter, *n* – someone who bets.

put down, *v* – used about an animal, it means to have it killed painlessly.

Q

quack, *n* – doctor. The term seems to stem from a defensive philistinism. In the days when the medical profession was unregulated, it meant an ignorant pretender to medical skill. It is still used in a similar sense for practitioners of alternative medicine.

quango, *n* – an acronym for quasi-autonomous non-governmental organization, a body funded by the government, sometimes with statutory powers, such as the Commission on Racial Equality and the Industrial Relations Tribunal.

quantity surveyor, *n* – a person who estimates the amount of materials required for a building.

quart, *n* – 69.35 cubic inches, against the American quart's 57.75 cubic inches (liquid).

quaver, *n* – eighth note. Musical.

Queen's Counsel, *n* – an honorary rank for a barrister (see BARRISTER), signified by the letters 'QC' after his name. Becoming a QC is known as taking silk. When a king is on the throne, the QC becomes a KC.

queer, *adj* – in addition to its colloquial derogatory meaning of homosexual, this can also mean 'unwell'. This is working-class, and more Northern than Southern. Soon after arriving in England after an American upbringing, I was told one day, in a friendly tone, 'You're looking a bit queer today, lad.' I said apologetically, 'Oh really? Perhaps it's this suit.'

queue, *n* and *v* – a line of people waiting, or, as a verb, to wait in line. A Dutchman of my acquaintance, arriving at London Airport, was waiting at a pay station to make a call and was baffled when someone asked him, in all seriousness, 'Are you the queue?' When this was interpreted and they decided between them that he was, the man fell into place behind him to wait his turn.

quid, *n* (col) – £1, a pound sterling.

R

rabbit, *v* (col) – to talk, chat. Cockney rhyming slang (rabbit-and-pork – talk).

racecourse, *n* – racetrack.

Rachmanism, *n* – slum landlord practices. The word comes from the name of a notorious slum landlord who received a great deal of attention at one point because he was a member of the Christine Keeler–Mandy Rice-Davies circle.

RADA, *prop n* (abbr) – the Royal Academy of Dramatic Art, the leading British drama school.

rag, *n* – student revelries, characterized by boisterousness and stunts. At some colleges and universities, this is formalized in a 'rag week'.

rag, *v* – to tease, josh.

rag-and-bone man, *n* – junk man.

railway, *n* – railroad.

ramp, *n* – a swindle, or a falsehood spread to make someone a profit.

randy, *adj* – horny, sex-hungry.

rasher, *n* – a slice of bacon.

rates, *n* – local property taxes.

rating, *n* – an enlisted man in the Royal Navy.

rave-up, *n* (col) – a youthful rock party.

Rawlplug, *prop n* – a small plug inserted in a wall as a fixing for a screw, similar to a Mollybolt. A trade name now used widely.

reader, *n* – a kind of assistant professor.

ready or **readies, the,** *n* (col) – money.

reception, *n* – in a hotel, the front desk. The **reception clerk** is the room clerk.

reception centre, *n* – a center established by the local authorities for homeless families.

reception room, *n* – a living or dining room. An ad for an apartment might say '3 beds, 2 recep. rooms'.

recorder, *n* – a judge in a lower court.

redbrick, *n* – referring to the older universities other than Oxford, Cambridge and London.

redcap, *n* – military policeman.

reef knot, *n* – a square knot.

reel, *n* – a spool of cotton, wire, tape, etc.

Reform Jew, *n* – roughly similar to a Conservative Jew.

Regency, *prop n* and *adj* – the style or fashion of the period 1810–20, when the future King George the Fourth was Prince Regent. 'Architecturally, some of Brighton's streets are still Regency streets' – a tourist board guide.

registrar, *n* – a senior doctor in

a hospital, ranking just below a consultant.

Remembrance Sunday, *prop n* – Veterans' Day.

reserve price, *n* – upset price at an auction.

re-sit, *v* – to take an examination for the second time.

return, *adj* – round-trip. One buys a **return ticket** in Britain.

revise, *v* – to study for an exam, going over material already learned.

rhubarb, *v* – to murmur, as an actor in a crowd, in order to create an impression of hub-bub. The traditional way is to murmur the word 'rhubarb'.

rhyming slang, *n* – a complex Cockney slang system, almost a tribal code, in which a phrase or, more usually, the first part of a phrase, is used to stand for a word that rhymes with it. For instance, 'head' becomes 'loaf of bread', or, these days, 'loaf'; 'look' becomes 'butcher's hook' shortened to 'butcher's'.

ringroad, *n* – beltway.

rise, *n* – a raise in salary.

rissole, *n* – a fried cake of minced food, usually leftovers.

rock cake, *n* – a small cake with a rough surface containing currants.

rocket, *n* (col) – a strong telling-off.

rock salmon, *n* – dogfish.

roger, *v* (col) – to screw, have sexual intercourse with.

rollmop, *n* – pickled herring bottled in rolled-up shape.

roll neck, *adj* – turtle neck.

ropey, *adj* (col) – in bad condition, wobbly, 'on the ropes'.

rotovator, *n* – a power-driven tool with rotating blades that breaks up and sifts the soil.

Rotten Row, *prop n* – the bridle path in London's Hyde Park set aside for horseback riding.

rotter, *n* – a term of abuse, strictly speaking a rotten person. An upper-class word, which is also public school (in the British sense) slang.

round, *n* – a delivery route, as in **milk round, newspaper round**, etc. Also **roundsman**, *n* – any delivery man with a regular route.

roundabout, *n* – 1. traffic circle. 2. carousel.

rounders, *n* – a children's game similar to stickball, a crude version of baseball.

rowing boat, *n* – rowboat.

royal circle, *n* – mezzanine in the theater.

rozzer, *n* (col) – policeman. Working-class.

rubber, *n* – eraser. A lady who is now deputy headmistress of a London school spent some time teaching in California, and once told a class going in for a geometry exam to be sure to have rubbers with them since anyone can make a mistake. She couldn't understand why this broke them up.

rubbish, *v* – to trash, in the verbal sense, bad-mouth. 'He rubbishes it and compares it unfavourably with the Channel Four rival production.' – from the *Guardian*, April 6, 1983.

ruddy, *adj* (col) – an all-purpose adjective, synonymous with 'bloody'.

rugby, *n* – a game superficially similar to American football in that it is played with the same shape ball and the object is to carry it to the end zone, but with many differences, including the size of the team, fifteen. Sometimes called **rugger**. It got its name because it originated in Rugby School.

rum, *adj* – odd, curious.

rumble, *v* – to find out about something, learn a secret.

runner beans, *n* – French beans.

run-up, *n* – a period of preparation for an event. From cricket, where the **bowler** takes a run before bowling the ball.

rural dean, *n* – a Church of England clergyman with authority over several parishes, ranking just below an archdeacon.

rusticate, *v* – to suspend a student from a college or university.

S

saloon, *n* – sedan car.

saloon bar, *n* – one of the two or more bars into which most pubs are divided, in class terms slightly superior to the public bar.

salt beef, *n* – corned beef.

Samuel Smiles, *prop n* – the Victorian author of a book called *Self Help* which preached the virtues of self-improvement, upright behavior, etc. He is often cited as the epitome of complacent Victorian-type attitudes.

Sandhurst, *prop n* – the army academy, Britain's West Point.

sandpit, *n* – sandbox.

sanitary towel, *n* – sanitary napkin.

sarkey, *adj* (col) – sarcastic, bitter-tongued.

sarnie, *n* – sandwich.

sassenach, *n* – the Scottish term for an Englishman; originally the Gaelic word for 'Saxon', it is now used facetiously more often than not.

saveloy, *n* – a highly-seasoned sausage.

Savile Row, *prop n* – the street in London that contains most of the top tailors, hence the term for high-class expensive tailoring.

savoury, *n* – a course in a meal, a light tasty dish occasionally offered instead of a dessert.

savoy, *n* – a cabbage with a large close head and wrinkled leaves.

scale, *n* – a schedule of professional fees laid down by statute or by a professional body, like certain lawyers' and architects' fees.

scarper, *v* (col) – to run away. Cockney rhyming slang, from Scapa Flow (a naval base in Scotland) – go.

scent, *n* – perfume. Both words are used.

schooner, *n* – a large sherry or port glass, hence much smaller than an American schooner.

scoff, *v* (col) – to gobble down, eat.

scone, *n* – a light, plain, small cake, usually eaten hot and with butter, with a distinctive flavor. Traditional tea-time fare.

Scot, *n* – the correct name for a native of Scotland. **Scottish** is the adjective to describe things that come from there. **Scotch** should be used only about the whisky, strictly speaking, though this is not always adhered to, as the term that follows shows.

Scotch egg, *n* – a hard-boiled egg encased in fried sausage meat. A favorite cold snack in pubs.

Scotland Yard, *prop n* – the headquarters of the Metropolitan (i.e. London) police, often used as a synonym for the force. It used to be located on a tiny street off Whitehall called New Scotland Yard; it occupied the entire street. Now it is in a modern building about half a mile away, but has kept the same name.

scouse, *n* and *adj* (col) – referring to Liverpool, or someone who comes from there. It also means a stew eaten locally and it derives from this.

scrag end, *n* – the cheap end of a piece of meat.

scraggy, *adj* – meagre, scrawny.

screw, *n* – a salary. An Englishman who says he is getting a good screw is only talking about money.

screw, *v* (col) – to extract money from.

scrimshank, *v* – to shirk.

scrubber, *n* – a scruffy girl who sleeps around. A term of contempt.

scrum, *n* – the moment in rugby (see RUGBY) when the forwards of the two teams, heads down, all push against one another. Occasionally used of social situations resembling this.

scrump, *v* – to pilfer fruit from fruit trees.

scrumpy, *n* – rough country cider.

scrutineer, *n* – a canvasser of votes.

scullery, *n* – a room off the kitchen in large, old-fashioned houses for rough cleaning work.

scupper, *v* (col) – to ditch, sink or cause to fail, e.g. 'That's scuppered our plans.'

SDP, *prop n* (abbr) – Social Democratic Party (see).

season ticket, *n* – commuter ticket.

secateurs, *n* – a scissors-like cutting instrument for pruning.

second, *v* – to assign to other work temporarily, e.g. 'He was in the Foreign Office, but was seconded to the Prime Minister's office for a year.' The accent is on the second syllable. As a noun, it becomes **secondment.**

secondary modern school, *n* – until recently, this was the less academic of the two kinds of schools into which most of Britain's secondary education was divided. Now they have been abolished in the reorganization of public education.

select committee, *n* – a House of Commons committee that oversees certain areas of government. It takes evidence, but does not consider bills, and does not have the role of a Congressional committee in the legislative process.

Sellotape, *prop n* – transparent adhesive tape. Like Scotch Tape, this is a trade name that has become a generic term.

semi-breve, *n* – whole note. Musical.

semi-detached or **semi,** *n* and *adj* – see DETACHED.

seminary, *n* – in Britain this means a college for training Roman Catholic priests. It is not used about any other denomination.

semi-quaver, *n* – sixteenth note. Musical.

semolina, *n* – the large, hard part of wheat grains, used for making puddings.

send down, *v* – to expel or suspend from university.

send up, *v* – to mock or parody. Sophisticated slang, theatrical, etc.

senior service, *n* – the Royal Navy. Also sometimes called the **silent service**.

service flat, *n* – a rented apartment which is cleaned and serviced.

serviette, *n* – napkin. Alan Ross (see Introduction) says it is non-u.

Seville orange, *n* – a bitter orange used only to make marmalade or in cooking.

shadow cabinet, *n* – the leaders of the opposition party in Parliament, who would form the cabinet if the opposition gained power. Members each have their area of responsibility, so that there is a shadow foreign secretary, a shadow defense minister, and so on.

shakedown, *n* – a makeshift bed for the night.

shandy, *n* – a thirst-quenching drink consisting of beer mixed with either lemonade or ginger beer (a soft drink).

shares, *n* – stocks. Though Britons speak of the stock exchange and a stockbroker, it's **shares, shareholder** and the **shares market**.

shemozzle, *n* (col) – fight, row.

shepherd's pie, *n* – a pie of ground meat covered with potato. 'If violence is as American as cherry pie, abhor-rence of violence is certainly as English as shepherd's pie.' – from *The Londoners* by W.H. Nelson.

sherbet, *n* – a powdered candy with a sherbet flavor.

shilling, *n* – obsolete, strictly speaking, since decimal coinage was introduced in 1971, this refers to the coin that is now 5 pence (it was 12 pennies under the old system); the word is still used.

shire, *n* – a county, usually applied to the rural aspect, and particularly **the shires**, Midland counties seen as fox-hunting country.

shirty, *adj* (col) – huffy.

shoot, *v* – to hunt with a gun. An Englishman will say, 'I went shooting yesterday.'

shooting brake, *n* – a station wagon with a large space at the back for luggage.

shooting match, whole, *n* (col) – the works, the whole lot.

shop, *n* – store. **store** is used only for a department or general store.

shop, *v* (col) – to turn someone over to the police. Mostly an underworld term.

shop assistant, *n* – sales clerk.

shop-fitter, *n* – a person who instals furnishings and display equipment for a store.

shop steward, *n* – the n.c.o.s of the labor unions, elected by the men on the factory floor to look after their interests.

short, *n* – in a pub, this means a drink of spirits as opposed to beer.

shorthand typist, *n* – stenographer.

short list, *n* – a reduced list of

possibilities, used mostly about applicants for a job who remain as candidates after others have been eliminated.

shorts, *n* – short pants, never underwear.

shout, *n* – a call for a round of drinks. 'It's my shout' means 'It's my turn to buy the drinks'.

shove-halfpenny, *n* – a traditional pub game, rarely found in towns these days, in which the players skid a coin along a board. Pronounced 'shove-haypenny'.

shower, *n* (col) – a stupid, disagreeable or otherwise inferior individual or collection of people. Officers' mess slang, usually said in traditional officers' mess accents.

shufti, *n* (col) – a look at something. An Arabic word brought back by the army. Heedless of the tautology, the services call some complex optical devices 'the shuftiscope'. Pronounced 'shoofti'.

shy, *v* – to throw at something. A **coconut shy** is a traditional fairground game in which you throw wooden balls at coconuts.

sick, *adj* – nauseous. To **be sick** means to throw up. It never means to be ill in any other way, though, illogically, Britons speak of **sick leave** and a **sick bed**.

side, *n* (col) – airs, a high-hat manner based on rank or position.

sideboards, *n* – sideburns.

silencer, *n* – muffler on a car.

silk, *n* – a lawyer who **takes silk** becomes a Queen's Counsel. See QUEEN'S COUNSEL.

silver plate, *n* – as well as electro-plate, this means solid silver eating utensils.

silverside, *n* – the top of a round of beef, usually salted.

single, *n* – one-way. Ask for a railroad ticket and you will probably be asked 'Single or return?'

single cream, *n* – table cream.

singlet, *n* – undershirt.

sink, *n* – kitchen sink. The one in the bathroom is a 'basin'.

SIS, *n* – Secret Intelligence Service: see MI6.

sister, *n* – a head nurse.

sitting tenant, *n* – a tenant whose right to remain is guaranteed by law.

six, *n* – in cricket, when the ball is hit out of the field, so that it would be a homer in baseball, it counts for six runs. Hence, to **hit** (someone or something) **for six** is to score a resounding success.

six of the best, *n* – a spanking. A public school (in the British sense) term.

skate, *n* – ray. This is eaten in Britain, and is often the fish in fish and chips.

skedaddle, *v* (col) – scram, beat it. A schoolboy word. Pronounced 'skeedaddle'.

skinhead, *n* – a young man with close-cropped hair, suspenders and boots, which supposedly advertise a liking for thuggery.

skint, *adj* (col) – flat broke.

skirting board, *n* – baseboard.

skivvy, *n* – a maid, particularly one who does rough work.

skyve or **skive,** *v* (col) – shirk, loaf on the job.

slag, *n* (col) – a girl or woman who is coarse and of ill-repute.

slag, v (col) – to bad-mouth. Newish, youthful.

slash, n (col) – the act of urinating, e.g. 'I'm going for a slash.'

slate, n (col) – credit, e.g. 'Put it on the slate.'

slate, v – to criticize severely.

sleeper, n – a railroad tie.

sleeping partner, n – silent partner in a business. The term is being replaced by the American one more and more, because of its obvious ambiguities.

sleeping policeman, n – obstruction in the road to slow down traffic.

Sloane Ranger, n – an upper-class girl, or sometimes young man, whose social life in London is centered geographically around Sloane Square (the family always has a country home); the term denotes a life-style, and was coined by the British journalist Peter York, whose speciality is observing life-styles. Princess Diana was an exemplary Sloane Ranger before she married.

slog, n and v – hard, plodding work; as a verb, it means to persevere with this.

slow coach, n – slow poke.

small beer, n – something of little account. The term has a long past, viz. Shakespeare: 'She was a wight ... to suckle fools and chronicle small beer.' – from *Othello*.

smalls, n – men's or women's underwear. The word is slightly dated.

smoke, the, n (col) – London, to people in central and Northern England.

snakes and ladders, n – the commonest children's dice and board game. Because the counters, on their way to the goal, zip up ladders with good luck or down snakes with bad luck, it is often used in the construction of metaphors.

snap, n – a children's card game played with picture cards in which a player calls out 'Snap!' when two of the same kind appear. Hence in English speech, a cry of 'snap' means that something has been discovered identical with something else, e.g. in the British movie *Live Now, Pay Later*, two girls talking about a local Lothario: 'What happened when you went out with him?' 'What do you think?' 'Snap.'

snifter, n – a small drink.

snip, n – bargain.

snog, v (col) – to neck.

snooker, n – a kind of pool game.

snuff it, v (col) – to die. This also goes back to Shakespeare: Wolsey, in *Henry VIII*, says 'Tis I must snuff it.'

Social Democratic Party or **SDP,** *prop* n – a major political party founded in 1981 by some leading figures from the moderate wing of the Labour Party. Like the Liberal Party, with which it currently has an electoral alliance (see ALLIANCE), it stands ideologically between the Labour and Conservative Parties.

sod, n and v – a term of abuse: 'You sod!' is roughly equivalent to 'You bastard!' As a verb, it is dismissive: 'Sod it!' means 'Screw it!' It is also used occasionally as an adjective, e.g. 'this sodding job'.

Soho, *prop n* – a small area of central London devoted mostly to strip clubs, restaurants and other forms of night life.

solicitor, *n* – a lawyer who usually handles the out-of-court work. A lawyer who appears regularly in court is a barrister, although under recent changes a solicitor can now appear before most courts.

Solicitor General, *prop n* – the government's law officer, who can prosecute on behalf of the government. Next in rank to the Attorney General.

solo, *n* – two-handed whist.

soppy, *adj* (col) – silly. A childish word.

sorbet, *n* – sherbet. A smart dinner-table word; it would not refer to something sold on a stick. Pronounced the French way, 'soorbay'.

sort out, *v* – 1. to work something out. 2. (col) to beat up.

spanner, *n* – monkey wrench.

spare, *adj* (col) – distraught, or hopping mad.

spatula, *n* – doctor's tongue depressor; it means the kitchen utensil also.

Special Branch, *prop n* – the branch of Scotland Yard (see SCOTLAND YARD) that deals with political crimes such as terrorism.

SPG, *prop n* (abbr) – Special Patrol Group, a unit of the London police that deals particularly with violent or potentially violent situations, including political demonstrations that might turn nasty.

spiffing, *adj* – splendid, excellent. Dated, upper-class, and used today almost only for comic effect.

spigot, *n* – the winding part of a faucet, never the whole faucet, as in America.

spinster, *n* – dated term for an unmarried woman. Some fresh-faced American girls in Britain are even now occasionally surprised to see themselves legally described as spinsters.

spit and polish, *n* (col) – smartness on parade.

spiv, *n* (col) – originally a wartime term meaning a small-time black marketeer, it means now a sharp, flashy person who lives by petty dishonest dealings. The adjective **spivvy** means a sharp, flashy way of dressing that implies this character.

spliff, *n* (col) – marijuana. A word brought in from Jamaica.

sponge bag, *n* – a waterproof bag for toilet articles.

spot-on, *adj* (col) – on the button, just what's needed.

sprat, *n* – a very small fish like a miniature herring. 'Use a sprat to catch a mackerel' is a common folk saying, meaning to give something in the expectation of getting something more in return.

spring greens, *n* – young cabbage.

spring onion, *n* – scallion.

squaddy, *n* (col) – soldier. Working-class.

squadron leader, *n* – a rank in the RAF equivalent to major.

square-bashing, *v part* (col) – military drill.

square dress hook, *n* – L hook.

squash, *n* – a soft fruit drink, not carbonated.

squiffy, *adj* (col) – a little drunk; a genteel term. During the First World War political crisis in Britain, the coterie of Liberal Party politicians who supported Prime Minister Asquith were known as the 'squiffites'; there is disagreement about whether this was a corruption of Asquith's name or a reference to his fondness for liquor.

SRN, *n* (abbr) – state registered nurse.

stag, *n* – in the financial world, someone who buys new stocks and sells them again for a quick profit. It's also a verb, **to stag.**

stalls, *n* – the ground floor in a theater.

stand, *v* – a politician stands for office in Britain, instead of running for office.

standard lamp, *n* – floor lamp.

starkers, *adj* – stark naked.

starters, *n* – the first course of a meal. An informal word.

state, *n* and *adj* – pertaining to the national government. In political discussion, it often means the opposite of what it would in America. For instance, a demand for more state control in a certain area is a demand for *more* state power for the central government.

Statute of Westminster, *prop n* – the statute passed in 1931 which ratified the independent status of the Dominions, and is a sort of constitution of the Commonwealth.

STD, *n* (abbr) – subscriber trunk dialling (see TRUNK), the system by which a telephone subscriber makes a long distance call by dialling it rather than going through the operator.

steps, *n* – a household ladder. A Briton will say, 'I'll get the steps and climb up there.'

stick, *n* (col) – abuse, as in 'He's getting a lot of stick because of what he said.'

sticky, *adj* (col) – difficult or dangerous. A **sticky wicket** (see WICKET) is a difficult situation.

stocks, *n* – bonds. This, at any rate, is the correct use of the word in Britain, but it is occasionally used more loosely to refer to equity shares, as it would be in America.

stodge, *n* – heavy, unappetizing food.

stone, *n* – 1. 14 lb, a measure of a person's weight. 2. the pit of a fruit.

stony or **stony broke,** *adj* (col) – flat broke. A 1930s upper-class term that lingers on here and there.

stop-go, *n* – government policies that alternate erratically between economic expansion and contraction.

store, *n* – department store. Any other kind is a **shop.**

stout, *n* – a dark, sweetish beer.

stream, *v* – to divide students into streams according to their ability.

stroke, *n* – slash. 1/2 is spoken as 'one stroke two'.

stroppy, *adj* (col) – belligerent, looking for trouble.

student union, *n* – an organization, well-established and financed at most British universities, that runs many non-academic canteen activities. It also means the building, which often includes a canteen and bar.

stuff, *v* (col) – to screw. An American girl I know brightened up a party in London when, arriving after supper, she refused food saying, 'I've just been stuffed.' 'Get stuffed!' means 'Go to hell!'; 'Stuff it!' means 'To hell with it!'

stump, *v* – baffle, puzzle. Normally used only in the passive, e.g. 'I'm stumped'.

sub, *n* – an advance on wages, or *sub*vention.

subaltern, *n* – a second-lieutenant.

sub-editor, *n* – a person on a newspaper who combines the functions of copy-reader and rewrite man (neither of these terms is used in Britain).

subject, *n* – citizen of Britain. Britons speak of a 'British subject', though an 'American citizen'.

subs, *n* – subscription, dues.

subway, *n* – an underground passage across a busy road. It does not mean an underground train system.

sultana, *n* – a large raisin.

sunblind, *n* – a sunshade over a window.

sundowner, *n* – an evening drink. A word brought back from the tropical colonies.

superannuated, *adj* – old-fashioned; or unfitted to hold a job because of age.

superannuation scheme, *n* – retirement pension scheme.

supergrass, *n* – see GRASS.

supertax, *n* (col) – surtax on high incomes.

supplementary benefit, *n* – welfare payments, usually in addition to pension or other benefits, where these do not provide enough money to live on.

supply teacher, *n* – substitute teacher.

supremo, *n* – a supreme commander, usually military or in administration.

surgery, *n* – a doctor's office. It also means the period during which a doctor sees patients, e.g. 'He has a surgery in the mornings and most afternoons.' A Member of Parliament or local councillor also speaks of his 'surgery', meaning his time for seeing constituents who bring their problems to him.

surrounds, *n* – the baseboard in a house plus the edges of doorways and windows.

suspenders, *n* – sock or stocking suspenders only. The other kind are **braces.**

suss, *v* (col) – suspect. A term that has come up from the underworld in the last few years. **suss out** means either to reconnoitre a situation or to sniff out something: e.g. 'Thought you'd get away with it, didn't you, but I sussed out.'

swan, *v* (col) – to live it up at someone else's expense, to go junketing.

swan upping, *n* – an expedition to seize young swans and mark their beaks with a sign of ownership.

swedes, *n* – yellow turnip; the word actually stands for 'Swedish turnip'.

sweet, *n* – 1. dessert. 2. a piece of candy. **sweets** means candy.

sweet Fanny Adams, *n* – see FANNY ADAMS.

sweetshop, *n* – candy store.

swingeing, *adj* – huge, as in a 'swingeing new tax'.

swing it, *v* – short for 'swing the lead' (see LEAD).

swish, *adj* – fancy, elegant.

swiss roll, *n* – jelly roll.

switch, *n* – 1. a piece of false hair that is attached to a woman's hair to make it longer. 2. a point on a railroad.

switchback, *n* – a fairground ride on an undulating track.

swot, *v* and *n* (col) – to work hard at studies. Used as a noun, it means a grid.

T

ta, *interj* (col) — thank you. Cockney.

ta-ta, *interj* (col) — good-bye. Working-class.

table, *v* — in parliamentary language, this means to put down for discussion, the exact opposite of the American meaning, to set aside. At a recent disarmament conference, the American and British delegations spent a large part of an afternoon locked in argument about whether to table a certain British motion before they found out they were on the same side. The Americans kept saying, to the Britons' confusion, 'But it's a very *good* motion. Why do you want to table it?'

tablespoon, *n* — as a measure, five-eighths of a fluid ounce, slightly more than an American.

Taffy, *n* (col) — a Welshman.

tailboard, *n* — tailgate. It is not used as a verb.

take-away, *adj* — take-out, as in **take-away food**.

take on, *v* (col) — to display great excitement or emotion, e.g. 'Oh, don't take on so over such a small thing.'

tallboy, *n* — high boy, the piece of furniture.

tally clerk, *n* — a clerk who checks a ship's cargo against a list.

tallyman, *n* — a man who sells things from door to door, and collects payment by instalments.

tanked up, *adj* — drunk.

Tannoy, *prop n* — a brand of public address system that has come to stand for any kind.

taproom, *n* — a bar in a hotel.

tart, *n* — 1. an open pie. 2. prostitute; a loose term for it, often denoting character as well as profession. A well-known English bar-room verse goes:

> It nearly broke the family's heart
> When Lady Jane became a tart;
> But they clubbed together and
>   bought her a beat
> On the sunny side of Jermyn Street.

tart up, *v* (col) — to prettify.

tat, *n* — a small object that is shabby, tawdry or worn. In the theater it means an actor's accessories. **tatty,** as an adjective, means shabby, tawdry.

tea, *n* — as well as a beverage, a meal. Among the middle and upper classes, a mid-afternoon snack accompanied by tea; among the working classes, the meal the man has when he comes home from work, his supper. See HIGH TEA.

tea leaf, *n* (col) — thief. Cockney rhyming slang.

tearaway, n (col) – a young tough.

teaspoon, n – as a measure, one-fifth of a fluid ounce, slightly more than an American.

teat, n – the nipple on a baby's bottle. (See NIPPLE).

tea towel, n – dish towel.

telephonist, n – telephone operator.

teleprinter, n – teletypewriter.

telly, n (col) – television.

temp, n (abbr) – a temporary secretary or typist, hired out by an agency.

ten-pin bowling, n – bowling.

terrace, n – a row of houses joined together. A **terraced house** is one of such a row of houses.

terraces, n – the open stands in a football stadium.

territorials, n – the **territorial army,** or **TA,** part-time reserve soldiers.

test or **test match,** n – an international cricket event.

tetchy, adj – peevish, touchy.

thick, adj – stupid, thick-headed.

thrash, n (col) – party. Upper-class.

through, conj – connected on the telephone. If a British telephone operator asks, 'Are you through?' she means 'Are you connected to your party?' not 'Are you finished?'

thump, v – hit. Overheard in an East End pub:
'Wotcher, mate. What you been doing lately?'
'Three months for thumping a copper.'

tick, n (col) – credit, as in the phrase 'The shop gave it to me on tick.'

tick, n and v – a check mark. A form might say, 'Please tick where appropriate.'

ticket barrier, n – the entrance to a railroad station platform or similar beyond which you cannot go without a ticket.

tick off, v (col) – to tell off.

tick over, n – of a car's engine, it means to run with the gears disengaged; hence, in any activity, to go on operating but without making any progress. 'The business is ticking over at the moment' means it's paying its costs but not making a profit.

tic tac man, n – a man at a race track who (quite legitimately) keeps the on-track bookmakers informed of the changing odds by hand signals.

tiddler, n – a very small minnow or stickleback; colloquially, it means a very small child, particularly one who is undersized.

tiddly, adj (col) – a little drunk. A genteel, feminine term.

tied cottage, n – a cottage owned by a farmer and let to one of his farm workers for as long as he works for him.

tiffin, n – lunch. From the Hindi, the word still has the flavor of empire about it.

tights, n – hose or pantyhose.

tin, n – can, e.g. Britons talk of a 'tin of peaches' and a **tin-opener.** Also **tinned,** canned. But Britons speak of **canned music,** not 'tinned music', as Brian Foster points out in *The Changing English Language.*

tinker, n – a gypsy-like vagrant in Scotland and Ireland.

tinkle, n (col) – telephone call.

tip, *n* – a garbage dump.

tipstaff, *n* – an official in a law court who carries out certain court functions.

tipsy, *adj* (col) – slightly drunk. A feminine word.

titfer, *n* (col) – hat. Cockney rhyming slang (tit-for-tat).

toad-in-the-hole, *n* – sausages baked in a batter.

tod, *n* (col) – own, as in 'I was on my tod.' It derives from nineteenth-century rhyming slang, Tod Sloan (a famous jockey of the period) – own.

toff, *n* (col) – a swell, big shot.

toffee, *n* – taffy.

toffee-nosed, *adj* – stuck-up, effete. Northerners often use the term about Londoners, their pubs, food and la-di-da accents.

togs, *n* (col) – clothes. **togged-up,** *adj* – dressed for the occasion.

Tolpuddle Martyrs, *prop n* – martyrs of the British labor movement honored today, six farm workers of the village of Tolpuddle who were sent to a penal colony in 1834 for trying to form a union.

tombola, *n* – a lottery at a social function in which people buy tickets to win a prize.

ton, *n* – 2,240 lb. Sometimes, a 2,000 lb weight is called a short ton. A **tonne** is a metric ton, 1,000 kilograms, or 2,204.6 lbs.

ton-up or **ton,** a speed of 100 miles per hour, achieved by a motorcyclist. It is used by Hell's Angels types.

top-drawer, *n* – socially upper-crust.

top liner, *n* – a person or act heading the bill at a theater.

top up, *v* – to fill a vessel that is already half-full. One may, for instance, 'top up' a drink, or a car's gas tank.

torch, *n* – flashlight.

Tory, *n* – a member of the Conservative Party.

toss off, *v* (col) – masturbate.

tot, *n* – a measure of spirits.

tote, *n* – the equivalent of pari-mutuel, the racetrack's own betting system.

touchline, *n* – the side line in some sports.

tower block, *n* – a tall residential or office building.

town hall, *n* – the local government building of a city or borough.

trade union, *n* – labor union. The difference in terminology reflects a difference in labor organization. In Britain, unions are organized along craft lines rather than by industry. An electrician, a mechanic and a carpenter working alongside one another in a railroad repair depot will belong to different unions because they have different trades.

traffic warden, *n* – a uniformed official who checks for parking offences.

trainers, *n* – sneakers.

tram, *n* – streetcar.

transport café, *n* – a cheap eating-place on a highway used mostly by truck drivers.

transporter, *n* – a large truck that carries automobiles.

traveller, *n* – traveling salesman. Short for 'commercial traveller'.

treacle, *n* – like molasses only with a lighter flavor.

Treasury Bench, *prop n* – the bench in the House of Commons occupied by members of the cabinet.

trick cyclist, *n* (col) – psychiatrist. A service term.

trifle, *n* – a dessert consisting of sponge cake, custard, sweet things or fruit and, usually, sherry.

trillion, *n* – 1,000,000 billion, a million cubed. See BILLION.

tripe, *n* – a cow's stomach lining, prepared as food. Used colloquially, it means nonsense, a pack of untruths, and is rather stately and old-fashioned.

tripper, *n* – a person on a day's outing.

trolley, *n* – cart, in a number of usages, for instance, a supermarket cart or a tea cart.

trousers, *n* – pants. **pants** in Britain means underpants. See first page of the Introduction.

trunk call, *n* – a long-distance telephone call.

tt, *n* and *adj* (abbr) – teetotaller, teetotal.

tube, *n* – subway.

tub-thumping, *adj* and *n* – soapbox oratory.

TUC, *prop n* (abbr) – the Trades Union Congress, the national labor body.

tuck, *n* – candies and similar goodies for a schoolboy or schoolgirl. They are sent in a **tuck box** and sold at a **tuck shop**.

tumble, *v* – to discover suddenly the truth of a situation. Unlike 'rumble', this is usually used without an accusative object, e.g. 'Then I tumbled.'

turf accountant, *n* – bookmaker. A euphemism if ever there was one, this is the term they use to describe themselves.

turf out, *v* – throw out.

turn, *n* – an act in vaudeville, e.g. 'a star turn'.

turn it up, *interj* (col) – cut it out! stop it!

turn-up, *n* (col) – something unexpected.

turn-ups, *n* – trouser cuffs.

twee, *adj* – icky, self-consciously cute.

twig, *v* (col) – to realize the truth of a situation; similar to **tumble**.

twin set, *n* – a woman's sweater and cardigan to match.

twist, *n* – nervous flutter, as in the phrase **in a twist**.

twister, *n* – a liar or otherwise dishonest person.

twit, *n* – a spectacular fool.

twit, *v* – to tease, josh.

U

U certificate, *n* – the equivalent of a g rating in America, a license for the showing of a movie to anyone of any age.

UDI, *n* (abbr) – unilateral declaration of independence. This term was first used when Ian Smith's Rhodesian government declared UDI in 1966, and soon became part of the political vocabulary.

uncle, *n* (col) – a pawnbroker.

undercarriage, *n* – an airplane's landing gear.

underdone, *adj* – rare, about meat.

underground, *n* – subway.

unit trust, *n* – almost the same as a mutual fund.

unofficial strike, *n* – wildcat strike.

up-and-downer, *n* (col) – row.

upper circle, *n* – the gallery in a theater.

u.s., *adj* – useless. The initials stand for unserviceable, and it was an army term originally.

V

VAT, *prop n* (abbr) – **value added tax,** a complicated tax on products and services, that was first applied in the European Economic Community and introduced in Britain when Britain joined the Community.

VC, *prop n* (abbr) – Victoria Cross, the highest award for military bravery.

verge, *n* – the shoulder of a road.

vest, *n* – undershirt. An American vest is a 'waistcoat'.

vet, *n* (abbr) – veterinary surgeon. It never means a veteran.

vet, *v* – to check, to look over for soundness.

veteran, *n* – an old soldier or relic of long service. It never describes a young ex-serviceman.

vicar, *n* – a Church of England parish clergyman.

vice-chancellor, *n* – the administrative head of a university. The chancellor is a distinguished person, and it is an honorific post.

villain, *n* – crook. Mostly an underworld and police term.

v-t, *n* (abbr) – in television, videotape. In an American TV studio one would just say 'tape'.

W

waistcoat, *n* – vest.

walkabout, *n* – a meet-the-people stroll among a crowd by a royal personage or other very famous figure. The word was first used by the press in 1969 during Queen Elizabeth's tour of Australia, where it in fact means something very different: a solitary trek in the desert by an aborigine, part of a tribal initiation rite for aboriginal boys.

wallah, *n* (col) – the person concerned with something, e.g. **laundry wallah, accounts wallah.** The word is Hindi and has a sound of the old Empire about it, as do some of the ingenious applications, like **amen wallah** for clergyman and **pop wallah** for teetotaller.

wallop, *n* (col) – bitter beer.

wally, *n* (col) – conspicuous fool.

warden, *n* – the man in charge of a residential institution, but not a prison; or the principal of a college. The head of a prison is a **governor.**

warder, *n* – a prison guard.

Wardour Street, *prop n* – the street in Soho (see SOHO) that houses the offices of most film companies, hence synonymous with the British movie industry.

washing powder, *n* – soap powder.

wash up, *v* – wash the dishes.

water ice, *n* – a kind of frozen candy similar to sherbet.

wear, *v* – to stand for, put up with, as in 'If we impose this condition, will he wear it?'

weatherboard, *n* – clapboard.

Webb's lettuce, *n* – like an iceberg lettuce, but less crisp.

weir, *n* – a small dam across a river or stream; or else fence for catching fish which strains the water rather than blocking it.

wellingtons or **wellies,** *n* – high rainproof rubber boots, also known as gumboots.

Wendy house, *n* – a playhouse for a child. After the house built for Wendy in *Peter Pan.*

West End, *prop n* – the center of London, containing most of the major places of entertainment and big stores. Like most port cities, London spread out from the dock area, in East London, so what is now the center was, 150 years ago, its western end.

Westminster, *prop n* – the part of central London in which Parliament and the central organs of government are situated. The term is sometimes used to mean the center of government.

wet, *adj* – 1. limp, silly, ineffectual, in short, a drip. 2. a political term applied to some in the Conservative Party, it means faint-hearted in support for tough policies, particularly economic policies.

whack, *n* (col) – a share to pay, as in 'When we went out for the evening, he always paid his whack.'

whacking, *adj* – whomping.

whacko, *interj* – jolly good! splendid! Spoken in the accents of an (English) public school, and usually for comic effect.

whelk, *n* – a shellfish sometimes eaten as a snack and sold on pushcarts at the seaside.

whip, *v* (col) – steal.

whippet, *n* – a dog related to the greyhound. Whippet-racing is a sport in some parts of England.

whip-round, *n* (col) – a collection for a cause, worked up informally.

whisky, *n* – Scotch. This is what it is called. If any other kind of whisky is meant, this is specified.

Whitehall, *prop n* – the street in London leading from Trafalgar Square to the Houses of Parliament which contains most of the key ministries and the Prime Minister's official residence. The word is used often to mean the executive side of government, including the bureaucracy, as distinct from the legislature.

white paper, *n* – official government report, giving the policy like on a matter for parliamentary discussion.

white spirit, *n* – turpentine substitute.

Whitsun, *prop n* – the Pentecostal weekend. **Whit Monday** is a national holiday.

wholemeal, *n* – wholewheat.

wicket, *n* – in cricket, the three stumps behind the batsman which the bowler tries to hit with the ball. Also, the stretch of ground in front of it. A **sticky wicket** means, colloquially, any difficult situation.

wide boy, *n* – a professional cheat.

widgeon, *n* – a kind of duck.

wigging, *n* – a telling-off. Upper-class.

willie, *n* (col) – penis. Childish.

windcheater, *n* – windbreaker.

windscreen, *n* – windshield.

windy, *adj* (col) – frightened. Someone who is windy has **got the wind up**. Slightly dated schoolboy slang.

wing, *n* – the fender of a car.

winge, *v* – to complain whiningly.

winkle, *n* – a sea snail, a traditional working-class food, though much less common than it was. Its one-time popularity has produced the two terms that follow.

winkle out, *v* – to pry out, like extracting a winkle from its shell.

winkle pickers, *n* – the sharp-pointed men's shoes that were popular a few years ago and are still seen, named after a pointed instrument for getting winkles out of their shells.

wireless, *n* – radio. This word is old-fashioned now, but it is still heard occasionally. Some people objected to this word when it was first introduced; in the debate in parliament on the first Wireless Telegraphy Act in 1923, Lord Riddell asked, 'Why describe a thing as a negation?'

witter, *v* – to talk emptily. Used mostly in the present participle, i.e. 'He went wittering on.'

wizard, *adj* (col) – excellent, very good. The term is dated, smacking of the 1930s.

wog, *n* (col) – a non-white person, especially an Arab. The word is said to be an acronym of 'wily Oriental gentleman', but it is more likely that it is derived from 'golliwog', a black-faced doll (see GOLLIWOG). In some military circles in Britain in which global strategy is discussed intervention in the Third World is known as **wog-bashing**. British parochialism is often parodied with the phrase 'wogs begin at Calais'.

Women's Institute, *prop n* – an association of women in many small towns and villages, genteel in style.

wonky, *adj* (col) – broken, not in working order. Working-class.

woolly, *n* – a sweater or cardigan. A homey, grand-motherly term.

woolsack, *n* – a cushion stuffed with wool on which, in accordance with tradition, the Lord Chancellor (see LORD CHAN-CELLOR) sits in the House of Lords. The word is often used to mean the office of Lord Chancellor.

working party, *n* – a committee formed to carry out a specific, temporary function.

works, *n* – factory or plant.

work-to-rule, *n* – go-slow; actually, a disruptive labor tactic that consists of working rigidly according to the regulations.

wotcher!, *interj* (col) – Hello! howdy! Cockney.

WRAC, *prop n* (abbr) – Women's Royal Army Corps, equivalent to the WAC.

WRAF, *prop n* (abbr) – Women's Royal Air Force.

wrap up, *v* (col) – shut up.

WREN, *n* (abbr) – a woman in the Royal Navy. The word comes from the acronym of Women's Royal Navy.

wrinkly, *n* (col) – an older person. Used mostly by young people of the upper crust, Sloane Rangers (see SLOANE RANGER) and their ilk.

WRVS, *n* (abbr) – Women's Voluntary Service, a national organization that carries out relief and welfare work.

Wykehamist, *n* – an alumnus of Winchester, a leading public school (in the British sense) with a reputation for high academic and intellectual standards.

Y

Yankee, *n* (col) – 1. Yank. Britons do not make the geographical distinction between North and South, so that a visitor from, say, Louisiana or Georgia may be irritated to hear himself described as a Yankee. 2. at the race track, a parlay of eleven bets.

yard, *n* – a small paved area adjoining a house. If it has grass or plants it is called a garden, no matter how small.

y-fronts, *n* – men's tight shorts; the fly and crotch are in the shape of a Y.

yobbo, *n* – hooligan, a badly-behaved, low-class youngster.

yomp, *v* (col) – to go on a hard trek, walking a long distance usually carrying a load. This is a service term that was introduced to the public during the Falklands War, and looks like remaining.

Yorkshire pudding, *n* – a pudding made of unsweetened batter, traditionally eaten with roast beef.

Z

zebra crossing, *n* – a road crossing marked in black and white stripes where a pedestrian has the right of way at any time.

zed, *n* – zee, the last letter of the alphabet.

z-car, *n* – police patrol car.

zigger-zagger, *n* – a rattle, not a baby's but the kind waved to make a noise at a sporting event.

zizz, *n* (col) – snooze, nap.

ALSO . . .

British

American

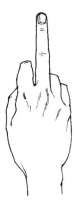

Useful subject lists

American/British

Accommodation
American plan
apartment
condominium
dinette
duplex apartment
duplex house
European plan
frame house
housing project
murphy bed
piazza
ranch house
tract home

Household
AC/DC
ash can
broiler
bureau
cheesecloth
cladding
clapboard
closet
clothes pin
coaster
colorwash
cookie sheet
cot
cotton
cup
cupboard
drapes
Dutch door
faucet

floor lamp
garbage
heater
highboy
kerosene
kettle
lowboy
lye
Mollybolt
pancake turner
plastic wrap
Saranwrap
shellac
shopping bag
sink
skillet
spool
tea cart
trimming
warming oven
wax paper
yard

Food
alligator pear
angel food cake
apple butter
baloney
beet
betty
biscuit
blueberry
blue point
brownies
buckwheat

Caesar salad
catsup
chef's salad
cherrystone clam
chicken à la king
chiffon
chipped beef
chuck steak
coffee cake
confectionery sugar
cookie
corn bread
corn dodger
corn pone
cornstarch
corned beef
crawfish
devil's food cake
dill pickle
disjoint
doughnut
eggplant
endives
English muffin
fig newton
finnan haddie
flapjack
french fried
french toast
fruit bread
fruit cup
graham cracker
griddle cake
grits
ground meat
ground round
half-and-half
hamburger meat
hard sauce
hero sandwich
hoagy
hominy grits
huckleberry
hush puppy
iceberg lettuce
jam
Jello

jelly
jelly roll
lima bean
limburger cheese
liverwurst
lox
maple sugar
molasses
mountain oyster
mulligan stew
oatmeal
oleo
oyster cocktail
parkerhouse roll
pecan
pemmican
persimmon
pop-over
porterhouse steak
pot roast
pound cake
powdered sugar
pumpkin
red-eye gravy
rib roast
rockfish
romaine lettuce
scallion
sherbet
shirr
short ribs
soda cracker
sowbelly
squash
succotash
sweet potato
table cream
taco
tamale
tart
tenderloin
tortilla
waldorf salad
weenie
whipping cream

Drink
applejack
bock beer
bourbon
branch water
chaser
cold duck
corn liquor
dago red
eggnog
float
highball
hooch
manhattan
martini
mint julep
mixer
old fashioned
rock and rye
rye
Scotch
straight up
suds
Tom Collins
white lightning

School and Campus
alma mater
alumnus
assignment
BMOC
college
commencement
fraternity
freshman
grade school
grind
gut course
high school
honors system
junior
junior college
normal school
parochial school
Phi Beta Kappa
preppy
prep school

public school
recess
regent
review
senior
sophomore
sorority
state university
tenure
theme

On the Road
auto
back-up lights
beltway
clearway
clunker
corduroy road
coupé
crosswalk
divided highway
expressway
fender
filling station
freeway
gear shift
hot rod
license plate
limit line
muffler
parking lot
parkway
pick-up truck
pull-off
sedan
speed zone
station waggon
throughway
traffic circle
trailer
trolley
trunk
turnpike
windshield

Clothes
bathrobe

beanie
capri pants
cut-offs
deck shoes
drawers
grubs
gumshoe
hose
jumper
knickers
lounge suit
mu-mu
nightgown
pants
pantyhose
pea jacket
pumps
rubbers
shorts
suspenders
sweatshirt
tennies
terrycloth
tights
tuxedo
undershirt
union suit
vest

Business and Finance
blue chip
bonds
bucket shop
building and loan association
certified check

chattel mortgage
checking account
commercial paper
common stock
Dun and Bradstreet
estate tax
fair trade
instalment plan
leverage
mutual fund
reserve bank
savings account

Politics
Administration
alderman
assembly
Bircher
caucus
congressman
district
gubernatorial
know-nothing
liberal
manifest destiny
mayor
mugwump
New Deal
open primary
plurality
pocket veto
pork barrel
selectman
smoke-filled room
unit-rule

British/American

Accommodation
bed-sitting room
block of flats
detached house
fixtures and fittings
flat
freehold
housing estate
maisonette
reception room
semi-detached
service flat
sitting tenant
terraced house

Household
airing cupboard
Anglepoise lamp
bath cube
carrier bag
chesterfield
chopper
cotton wool
cup
dessertspoon
drawing pin
dustbin
duvet
earth wire
eiderdown
fish slice
french polish
garden
geyser
greengrocer

gripewater
grocer
hob
ironmongery
loo
lumber room
mains
methylated spirits
Mrs Beeton
muslin
nappy
paraffin
primus stove
Rawlplug
scullery
·serviette
skirting board
tablespoon
teaspoon
teat
trolley
washing powder
white spirit
yard

Food
bap
banbury cake
bath bun
biscuit
bridge roll
broad beans
brussels sprouts
bubble and squeak
bun

butty
castor sugar
char
chicory
chipolata
chips
Christmas pudding
cockle
cornflour
cos lettuce
crispbread
crisps
crumpet
currant bread
digestive biscuits
double cream
doughnut
eccles cake
faggot
flan
flan case
fruit cup
gammon
gâteau
hake
hot pot
icing sugar
jacket potato
joint
kedgeree
kipper
lump sugar
marrow
mash
minced meat
mixed grill
pasty
patty
pease pudding
pie
plaice
porridge
prawn
rasher
rissole
rock cake
rock salmon

saveloy
savoury
scone
Scotch egg
Seville orange
shepherd's pie
silverside
single cream
skate
sorbet
sprat
spring greens
spring onion
squash
swiss roll
tart
toad-in-the-hole
treacle
trifle
tripe
winkle

Drink
bitter
brown ale
Burton
dram
egg flip
lager
light ale
Martini
pale ale
pink gin
plonk
scrumpy
shandy
small beer
stingo
stout
whisky

School and Campus
A-levels
Cantabrian
college
comprehensive school
county school

dormitory
eleven-plus
first
GCE
grammar school
headmaster, head
instructor
lines
matriculation
mistress
O-levels
Oxbridge
Oxonian
polytechnic
prefect
prep
prep school
primary school
proctor
professor
redbrick
re-sit
revise
rusticate
secondary modern
send down
Student Union
vice-chancellor
Wykehamist

On the Road
accumulator
big end
bonnet
box junction
breathalyser
caravan
central reservation
crash barrier
charabanc
coach
dual carriageway
estate car
filter sign
gear box
gear lever
hood

junction
lay-by
level crossing
L-driver
lorry
motorway
nearside
number plate
offside
petrol
ringway
tailboard
wing

Clothes
anorak
boater
boiler suit
braces
dinner suit
dressing gown
hacking jacket
jumper
knickers
long johns
lounge suit
mackintosh
nightdress
oilskin
pants
plimsolls
singlet
suspenders
tights
trousers
turn-ups
vest
windcheater
y-front

Business and Finance
assurance
chairman
current account
death duties
deposit account
director

gazump
gearing
gilt-edged
Giro
hire purchase
limited company
managing director
never-never
ordinary shares
overdraft
purchase tax
shares
stag
stocks
superannuation
supertax
unit trust
VAT

Politics
alderman
Alliance
back benches
caucus
Chancellor of the Duchy of
   Lancaster

Chancellor of the Exchequer
Chequers
Commons
Conservative Party
constituency
Downing Street
dry
front bench
Labour Party
Liberal Party
Lord Chancellor
Lord Privy Seal
Lords
mayor
Privy Council
Social Democratic Party
Statute of Westminster
surgery
Tory
Treasury Bench
UDI
Westminster
wet
Whitehall
Woolsack